Inside

steppe four

A CENTRAL ASIAN PANORAMA
SUMMER 2008

Cover Photograph: Holy Marker in the Taklamakan Desert, by Lisa Ross

steppe

A CENTRAL ASIAN PANORAMA

Publishers
Summer Coish
Lucy Kelaart

Editors
Summer Coish
Lucy Kelaart

Associate Editor
Mitchell Albert

Designer
Liz Dixon
liz@lizdixongraphicdesign.com

Cartographer
Matthew Rice

Translator
Ilona Chavasse

Proofreader
Brandon Hopkins

Printer
Wyndeham Grange, Southwick,
West Sussex

Colour Origination
PH Media, Roche, Cornwall

Special Thanks
Ian Claytor, Bessie Kelaart, Sue Meller,
Elena Tsareva, all our contributors and all
who have helped make STEPPE 4 possible

Subscriptions
One Year (Two Issues)
UK: £23 ($46) including p+p
US: £25 ($50) including p+p
Rest of World: £30 ($60) including p+p

Online subscriptions and back issues are
available at www.steppemagazine.com

Prices are charged in UK£ at the current
exchange rate

To subscribe by post, make cheques
payable to Steppe International Ltd

Send UK£ cheques to STEPPE, Manor Farm,
Nettlebed, Oxfordshire, RG9 5DA, UK

Send US$ cheques to STEPPE, PO Box 794,
Sullivan's Island, SC 29482, USA

Please include name, address, telephone,
email and the issue number from which you
wish the subscription to start

Advertising
Find out more about advertising in STEPPE at
www.steppemagazine.com/advertise or
email advertise@steppemagazine.com

Website
www.steppemagazine.com
Design, build and optimisation by
Metaphors: www.metaphors.co.uk

Sponsors
To learn about sponsorship opportunities,
please contact the Editors at
info@steppemagazine.com

Transliteration
Because there are numerous language
transliteration systems, we have employed
common usage for words and place names
that arise frequently. We call this the STEPPE
Transliteration System

Distribution
Distributed worldwide via subscription

Distributed in Central Asia by Polygon
International

Distributed in the UK, Europe and the US at
specialist shops

For more information on stockists, visit
www.steppemagazine.com/stockists

ISSN 1752-2412
ISBN 978-0-9555774-2-0

STEPPE is published by Steppe International
Ltd, Manor Farm, Nettlebed, Oxfordshire,
RG9 5DA, UK

The last thing I need at moments like this is the shakes.

When you're got nineteen hundred pounds of metal and wood bearing down on you at 200 mph, you're thankful for something solid beneath you.

Luckily, my Discovery can pretty much cope with any terrain and handles like it's on rails.

Well, why take any more risks than you need to?

DISCOVERY 3
TRUSTED BY EXPERTS

When
BALANCE
gives CONFIDENCE

KAZ
KOM

JSC Kazkommertsbank 135 zh, Gagarin Ave., Almaty, Kazakhstan 050060
tel.: +7 (727) 2585 471, fax:+7 (727) 2585 237 www. kazkommertsbank.com

KAZKOMMERTSBANK

Editors' Welcome

KAZAKHSTAN | KYRGYZSTAN | TAJIKISTAN | TURKMENISTAN | UZBEKISTAN | AFGHANISTAN | XINJIANG

DOMINATING CENTRAL ASIAN NEWS DURING THE LAST FEW months (and the focus of this issue's Dispatches column) was the region's particularly hard winter. Extreme cold and shortages of electricity and heating beset much of the region. So *Nauruz*, the Central Asian New Year, which celebrates the coming of spring, was even more welcome than usual. To share those celebrations with you, we travel to Tajikistan for the season's first *buzkashi* match (traditionally played at *Nauruz* across the region). Best described as a form of polo played using a goat carcass instead of a ball, *buzkashi* is one of Central Asia's main sports. It is so revered, and so much a part of local tradition, that matches and players alike tend to acquire cult followings.

Our main feature story takes advantage of the spotlight on China during this Olympic year to focus on the often overlooked Xinjiang province. We follow the paths of pilgrims deep into the heart of western China's Taklamakan Desert where everyday people visit the tombs and shrines of Sufi saints in search of well-being, fertility, love and spiritual guidance. The photographs will transport you into a world of pre-Islamic intensity, yet the desires underlying these pilgrimages are shared the world over.

Moving northwest of the Taklamakan to mountainous Kyrgyzstan, we encounter another type of pilgrimage where, every summer, locals flock to the shores of the pristine alpine lake of Issyk Kul. Why not partake in a bit of beachside rest and relaxation with this issue's STEPPE Guide in hand? The Guide provides details of what to do and see, as well as places to stay, including some old Soviet sanatoria – many of which have yet to undergo modern makeovers, thus preserving their unique Soviet feel.

If you are nostalgic for the Soviet past, our Top Ten section takes you on a tour of the many Lenin monuments that still stand tall today. Further afield, in Berlin, we visit the Tajik Teahouse donated by the Tajiks to the German Democratic Republic in the mid-1970s and still serving chai from its samovars. In Central Asia, the perfect accompaniment to tea (drunk with every meal) is a bowl of homemade noodles. This issue's Cookery feature teaches you how to knead, shape, cook and, of course, eat delicious Kazakh noodles, based on authentic recipes from western China.

Delving further back in time, we visit two exhibitions opening this spring that highlight the region's exquisite handiwork. In Washington, DC, some of Afghanistan's most magnificent treasures, dating back over 4,000 years, illustrate the country's immense cultural wealth that is otherwise virtually ignored in mainstream news coverage. In New York, we receive a rare glimpse of some of America's most prestigious private collections of Central Asian carpets and textiles, with many pieces that have never been shown publicly before.

Also in this issue, lose yourself in Jila Peacock's melodious Persian calligraphy shape-poems, which beautifully illustrate the place of poetry at the heart of Tajik culture. Spend a night in Kabul at Flashman's Gandamack Lodge, and enjoy our new watercolour map of Central Asia – specially drawn by artist and illustrator Matthew Rice for this issue. □

LK and SC

A True Story.

L'OCCITANE

VELOUTÉ DE RIZ
ULTRA-MATIFIANT
HYDRATE ET RÉÉQUILIBRE

RIZ
/
RICE

ULTRA-MATTE
FACE FLUID

MOISTURIZES* AND REBALANCES

ORIGINE
RIZ ROUGE BIO
CAMARGUE
ORGANIC RED RICE
ORIGIN

L'OCCITANE
EN PROVENCE

30ml - 1 Fl.oz.

ULTRA-MATTE FACE FLUID

MOISTURIZES*, MATTIFIES AND RESTORES

ORIGINE
RIZ ROUGE BIO
CAMARGUE
ORGANIC RED RICE
ORIGIN

RIZ
/
RICE

L'OCCITANE has created a skincare range using organic red rice from the Camargue in Provence. Red rice devotes its properties to the skin by providing rebalancing care. The ULTRA-MATTE FACE FLUID with its ultra-light, fresh and velvety texture moisturizes*, mattifies and restores balance to the skin all day long. Every day, the skin appears visibly clearer and smoother.

Effectiveness test**: • Immediate and long-lasting (8 hours) mattifying action.
• Rebalancing action: 18% average decrease of sebum on the surface of the skin.

Tolerance dermatologically tested. Non-comedogenic *Upper layers of the epidermis. **In-vivo test conducted on 26 subjects aged 20 to 45 years old.

ALMATY: 10 Satpaev Street +7 (727) 264 5344 • Ramstore-Samal 1st fl +7 (727) 258 2153
Promenade 1st fl +7 (727) 267 7447 • Silk Way City 1st fl +7 (727) 267 7523 • Mega Almaty 2nd fl +7 (727) 232 2524.
ASTANA: Sary-Arka, 1st fl +7 (7172) 97 42 41 • 18 Imanov Street +7 (7172) 22 13 78. AKTAU: Astana 2nd fl +7 (7292) 31 51 20.
AKTOBE: 70/1 Abulkhair Khan Avenue +7 (7132) 51 73 52. ATYRAU: Passage Nasikha 1st fl +7 (7122) 35 58 03

Dispatches

The Big Freeze

Joshua Abrams mulls over one of the coldest winters Central Asia has known, from which only Santa Claus – in his new home in Kyrgyzstan – came out smiling

PHOTOGRAPH BY ELENA SKOCHILO

CALL IT WHAT YOU WILL: FREAK WEATHER, global climate change, act of God. The killer frost that struck Central Asia this winter hit a region already burdened with difficulties. Temperatures throughout the region dipped well below −20 C as early as December and lasted well into February. Residents of desert oases, used to short, mild winters, found themselves buried under the snow, huddled in homes with no heat or light. The unexpected cold forced new levels of forbearance on the region's 60 million inhabitants, who have already seen food and fuel prices shoot up over the past year.

The winter revealed the raw helplessness of the region's governments in the face of real disaster. In bitter irony, even oil-and-gas giants, Kazakhstan and Turkmenistan, were paralysed by their own antiquated infrastructure. Death rates throughout the region for newborns, the elderly and the sick skyrocketed, as homes and even hospitals suffered prolonged energy cuts.

Kazakhstan did better than most, though only in the main cities. The country's many small towns and rural communities froze until spring, when massive floods deluged much of the south. Kazakhs could, at least, bathe in the warmth of international recognition, as the Kazakh-financed film *Mongol* made it to the Oscars. The epic biopic about Genghis Khan was nominated for Best Foreign Film. It did not win, but it brought no small amount of relief that a film that had nothing to do with Borat would finally be associated with the country. They also basked in the limelight as the first country to host the Olypmic torch. The flaming emblem of peace passed through Almaty without incident; it was only later that the torch became a symbol of protest against China.

Yet the good times seem to be coming to an end, at least for now. Kazakhstan's financial sector is being hit hard by the US sub-prime crisis, which in turn is affecting the country's booming real estate market. Builders such as the corporate giant Kuat have seen their credit dry up, leaving their many construction projects unfinished. The Kazakh economic boom has not included an expanding social security net, so as the building sector busts, the many thousands of people who purchased options on new flats find themselves with neither homes nor compensation.

President Nursultan Nazarbayev warned that the government will have to cut all but the most essential government services. Not included in the list of cuts, however, is Astana's ten-year anniversary celebration in July, an all-star gala with numerous events, A-list performers and red-carpet guests. Whether the thousands of homeless housing-crunch victims will also be invited is yet to be seen.

For all its woes, Kazakhstan joined Russia

'SANTA CLAUS, MEET SANTA CLAUS'
Santas from around the world gather on the frozen shores of Issyk Kul for the first-ever 'Santa Claus Summit'

and the West in offering aid to Tajikistan, which suffered the most this winter. The sustained cold kept the snow in the mountains, leaving the reservoirs dryer than usual, which reduced the amount of hydroelectric power generated. Expected fuel supplies from Uzbekistan and Kyrgyzstan were, unsurprisingly, also undelivered. Even Dushanbe suffered severe outages this year, while much of the rest of the country was cut off by the heavy snows.

Tajik President Emomali Rakhmon responded to the crisis by firing or reassigning various government ministers in January during a televised cabinet session that went unwatched due to power outages. Tajik officials admit the country is in shambles; with the severe weather boding ill for this year's harvest, what economy there is, is at a standstill. Aid is welcome, but donors should keep an eye on where the money goes. In March, the International Monetary Fund caught the Tajik government cooking its books, providing misleading economic information to win $47 million in loans. The Tajiks will have to pay the money back starting in September, though it is unclear where they will find the funds.

A BOOST TO [KYRGYZSTAN'S TOURISM INDUSTRY] CAME IN EARLY WINTER, WHEN SWEDISH EXPERTS IDENTIFIED A POINT IN THE KYRGYZ MOUNTAINS AS SANTA CLAUS'S BEST SPOT FOR A NEW HOME

Meanwhile, violence against Central Asian labour migrants in Russia continues unabated, with a number of Tajik workers killed even as Rakhmon was flying to Moscow in early March. Attacks on labour migrants in Russia have also became a national issue in Kyrgyzstan; a dozen nationals have been killed in Russia since January. The Kyrgyz parliament passed a resolution in February appealing to Russian lawmakers to address these attacks as hate crimes, while demonstrators in Bishkek also rallied to condemn the violence.

Industry-poor Kyrgyzstan exports hundreds of thousands of labourers to Russia each year, but the one sector set to keep growing is tourism. A boost to the industry came in early winter, when Swedish experts identified a point in the Kyrgyz Mountains as Santa Claus's best

cold. Local authorities responded to the protesters either with promises (usually empty) or punitive measures. Either way, the Uzbeks, too, spent the winter in the cold.

But with spring, Uzbekistan's frosty relations with the West are warming somewhat. A few political prisoners have been released, the usual sign of rapprochement, followed by a new agreement to open the Termez airbase to wider NATO use as an access point to Afghanistan. This will include American personnel, and while this is not the same as letting US forces back to the airbase at Karshi-Khanabad, it is still a hint that Karimov is looking to re-enter Western good grace, again.

Turkmenistan's international relations continue to improve, as President Gurbanguly Berdymuhammedov advances his agenda of

will lead to Afghanistan's descent into failed-state status. Increased attacks by the Taliban, including two February bombings in Kandahar that left hundreds of people dead, seem to bear out the report's prognosis. Another indicator is the poppy harvest, which is expected to boom again this year and is likely to result in enough cultivated opium to rival the estimated 9,000 tonnes yielded in 2007.

Even Afghanistan's *burqa* market is taking a beating as factories in China overtake the local cottage industries that traditionally produce the distinctive women's garment. While handmade *burqas* produced by Afghan tailors may sell for $20, the mass-produced Chinese versions can go for as little as $.20. Since China's entry into the market, hundreds of Afghan families have lost their businesses.

EVEN AFGHANISTAN'S BURQA MARKET IS TAKING A BEATING AS FACTORIES IN CHINA OVERTAKE THE LOCAL COTTAGE INDUSTRIES THAT TRADITIONALLY PRODUCE THE DISTINCTIVE WOMEN'S GARMENT

spot for a new home. Swedish consulting company SWECO based their calculations on optimising Santa's travel time, locating Kyrgyzstan as the best launching point to deliver presents most efficiently to the world's 2.5 billion households.

The Kyrgyz government immediately took advantage of the PR coup by holding the world's first-ever 'Santa Claus Summit' in February. Santas from around the world descended on the country for a festival of skiing, yak-riding competitions and present-giving. Given the energy cuts hitting Kyrgyzstan, it may be the first time children were asking Santa for a lump of coal.

Uzbekistan celebrated Christmas by re-electing President Islam Karimov in December 2007 to what may either be a technically illegal third term or technically legal second term, depending on how you count it. Karimov has made a career of overstaying his welcome, but perhaps the earthquake that hit the Ferghana Valley on New Year's Eve was a hint from above that, this time, he is really pushing it.

Other tremors were felt in Uzbekistan this winter as pockets of protesters hit the streets over the lack of gas in their homes. Civil disturbances were reported in several cities, from Ferghana to Karakalpakstan, as communities were driven to despair by the

finding friendly oil and gas customers without endangering the country's neutrality. At home, his agenda of mild domestic reform continues apace, and foreign culture – including opera, ballet, cinema and the circus – has been officially sanctioned once more. But Berdymuhammedov's honeymoon with his people seems to be over. The winter exacerbated the new petrol pricing policy he introduced last year in an attempt to slowly liberalise the Turkmen economy. Petrol and utilities were free under the president's predecessor – the people's reward for being kept in enforced poverty – and reforming the system without protest is proving difficult. The price hike is affecting everyone; bus and taxi fares have risen to meet petrol costs, which increased from $.08 to $.60 per litre, in a country with a median monthly income of $50. There is no chance of Turkmenistan falling apart over these reforms, but it is the first real challenge to the new president's regime and one that may define how Berdymuhammedov chooses to continue.

Falling apart is more of a risk in Afghanistan, and according to the Afghanistan Study Group Report, it seems a near certainty. The January report, published by the Center for the Study of the Presidency, a US think tank, warns that insufficient military and economic aid, combined with government corruption,

Despite their success in the *burqa* market, the Chinese have much to feel jittery about these days, too. The lead-up to the Beijing Olympics is bringing all sorts of international outcries – from the poor air quality for the games to the 'PR nightmare' of the latest Tibetan protests. Along with the Tibetans, China's Uighurs are feeling the brunt of Chinese security concerns. China's media has reported arrests of Uighur separatists accused of plotting terrorist attacks on the Olympics. News included raids in Urumqi, the capital of the Uighur homeland in Xinjiang, and the arrest of potential saboteurs on a flight from Urumqi to Beijing.

As always, the news is vague, the evidence sketchy and without free enquiry in China, there is no way to know whether the threat of separatism is really growing. The bugbear of Uighur separatism – labelled as Islamic militancy by the authorities – has long been used to justify security clampdowns in Xinjiang. Unlike the Tibetans, the Uighurs have no high-profile international spokesperson to highlight their problems, but perhaps the closer international scrutiny this Olympics year will finally put Xinjiang on the map.

The Olympics will, at least, provide a ready distraction from what has begun as a difficult year. The heavy winter is leading into a difficult spring, but at least spring brings the sun, warmth and more hours to the day. Spring also brings *Nauruz*, the New Year, with its promise of better times, easier days and a chance for growth and health and recovery – all very welcome after this harshest of winters. □

Joshua E. Abrams writes the *Dispatches* column for STEPPE. He enjoys visiting the local market near his Moscow apartment, where the friendly Tajik and Uzbek traders remind him of better days.

Snapshot

Waiting for Godot

Porters wait for clients at the edge of the Afrasiyab Bazaar in the centre of Samarkand, Uzbekistan. Today the large, spacious, partly open-air Afrasiyab Bazaar, named after the ancient city of Samarkand (destroyed by the Mongols in 1220 AD), lies at the heart of 'new' Samarkand. Row upon row of produce brought to market by local farmers fills the aisles, comprising dried fruits and nuts, herbs, spices, a colourful array of fresh fruits and vegetables including gigantic juicy melons, thick *lepioshka* (round flatbread), freshly butchered meat and a vast display of household goods.

As the porters wait for business, their backs are turned to the magnificent Bibi Khanum Mosque, commissioned by Timur (known in the west as Tamerlane) in 1398 as a *jama-e-masjid* (Friday Mosque) following his victorious campaign in Hindustan. The mosque was named after Timur's favourite wife, Sarai Mulk 'Bibi' Khanum, whose mausoleum lies opposite the imposing *iwan* (entrance portal) on the eastern side.

Ruy González de Clavijo, a Spanish traveller to Timur's court, described the Bibi Khanum Mosque – one of the largest buildings of its kind in the Islamic world – as 'the noblest of all those we visited in the city of Samarkand'. However, according to de Clavijo, Timur was dissatisfied with its size and progress, wishing it to be both grander and larger. Ultimately, the building was erected so hastily and made so large that not long after completion it began to crumble. The main *iwan* and the three domed structures within were restored from a ruinous state in 1974 by the Soviets.

Visible here, the remains of the external decoration attest to a varied and imaginative treatment incorporating mosaic faience, *haft rangi* tiles (tiles painted in seven colours), carved stone and *hazarbaf* (decorative) brickwork including *girikhs* (geometrical shapes) and gigantic Kufic inscriptions. Also visible is the domed chamber on the northern side (mirrored on the southern side), with a large, conical, ribbed dome decorated with the blue tiles for which Samarkand is famous. A third dome, just visible behind this one, stands at the western side of the mosque, providing cover for the *mihrab* (the niche indicating the direction of Mecca).

Despite its convenient position next to the bazaar, today the mosque is merely a shell – a monument to Timur and his architectural splendour. ☐

PHOTOGRAPH BY **TIM DIRVEN**

Afghan Treasures

Afghanistan's national treasures have been travelling the world in a bid to demonstrate the rich and diverse history of this country. **Fredrik Hiebert** catches up with them in Washington, DC.

AFGHANISTAN:
HIDDEN TREASURES FROM THE NATIONAL MUSEUM, KABUL
25 May – 7 September 2008
National Gallery of Art, Washington, DC
www.nga.gov

AFGHANISTAN, WHICH BOASTS SOME OF THE globe's richest archaeology, is permitting its national treasures to be viewed worldwide. These come from the collections of Afghanistan's fabled National Museum in Kabul, which was once renowned as one of the finest museums of Silk Road art. The museum hit hard times during the 1980s with the Soviet invasion and in the 1990s under the Taliban, during which time the museum was destroyed and all of its collections thought lost. It was incredible news for scholars and art lovers around the world when, in 2003, President Hamid Karzai announced the existence of several museum boxes hidden in the basement of the presidential bank vault in Kabul.

At that time, I went to Kabul to see if these boxes included the fabled Bactrian Hoard – a collection of thousands of gold objects from the excavations of ancient noble nomadic tombs from northern Afghanistan that had been part of the museum collections. The Afghan government offered to open the boxes provided a full scientific inventory be carried out along with personnel from the National Museum. Fifteen months later, the inventory was finished, and not only was the Bactrian Hoard safe and in excellent condition, but the same was true for most of the museum's masterpieces.

These amazing artefacts can now been seen in a travelling exhibition entitled 'Afghanistan: Hidden Treasures from the National Museum, Kabul', which highlights the rich cultural heritage of ancient Afghanistan from earliest times to the height of Silk Road trade in the first and second centuries AD.

The exhibition premieres in the US at the National Galley of Art in Washington, DC, from May until September 2008. On display are some 230 artefacts, including Bronze Age pieces dating back over 4,000 years, as well as hundreds of objects from the Bactrian Hoard.

The artefacts are drawn from four of the Kabul museum's archaeological collections. The first, from the site of Tepe Fullol, features several Bronze Age works including fragments of golden vases dated between 2500–2200 BC. The second collection was found at the site of the former Greek city of Ai Khanum and reflects the Mediterranean influence in the region between the fourth and second centuries BC. The items include ceramics, ivory and bronze figures and stone statues of Central Asian notables carved in a Hellenistic style. A third collection, comprising treasures from the site of Begram in central Afghanistan, dates from the first century AD and includes elaborate Indian ivory furniture, ivory statues and vases, bronzes and painted glassware, many imported from Roman, Indian, Chinese and East Asian markets.

The highlight of the exhibition, however, is the selection of objects from the Bactrian Hoard. Found at the site of Tillya Tepe ('The Golden Mound') in 1978 and hidden as soon as it was discovered, the Bactrian Hoard contains jewellery and gold ornaments from the graves of six Bactrian nomads dating from the first century AD. From a total of over 21,000 objects discovered there, a selection of exquisite necklaces, belts, buttons and headdresses – most made of solid gold with insets of local turquoise and garnets – will be on display.

Through text panels, short films, an audio tour and educational materials, visitors to the

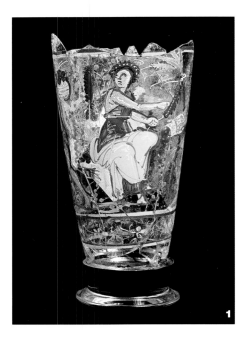

1 | A large glass beaker showing two male and two female figures between circular double-bands of yellow and ochre-red, from Begram, dating from the 1st century AD 2 | Male or female head made of unfired clay, dating from the 2nd century BC, from the site of the former Greek city Ai Khanum in a region of Afghanistan conquered by Alexander the Great 3 | Fragment of a gold bowl with Mesopotamian motifs, dating from the Bronze Age (2500 BC) from Tepe Fullol in northern Afghanistan 4 | A folding gold crown from a Bactrian nomad's grave discovered at Tillya Tepe in northern Afghanistan in 1978. The crown, dating from the 1st century AD and wrought of solid gold, was collapsible for easy transport 5 | Gilded silver disc showing the goddess of nature, Cybele, dating from the 3rd century BC, from the Temple of the Niches at Ai Khanum

exhibition will learn of the cultural significance and historical context of the artefacts, as well as the link between ancient and contemporary Afghanistan. They will also gain insight into how the artefacts survived the recent decades of war and chaos, and learn of the heroic Afghans who risked their lives to save these and other national cultural treasures from destruction by the Soviets and the Taliban.

The exhibition catalogue contains essays from some of the world's most renowned Silk Road scholars; in addition, photojournalists who have covered Afghanistan for decades present photo essays and explore major themes. A comprehensive exhibition website, hosted by National Geographic, will expand the experience online and feature a virtual tour, downloadable podcasts and interactive displays illustrating artefact details and telling the stories of key figures of the period such as Alexander the Great. □

'Afghanistan: Hidden Treasures from the National Museum, Kabul' will start its tour of the US in Washington, DC, and will then travel to the Asian Art Museum, San Francisco (24 October 2008 – 25 January 2009); the Museum of Fine Arts, Houston (22 February – 17 May 2009); and the Metropolitan Museum of Art, New York (15 June – 20 September 2009).

Fredrik Hiebert is National Geographic's Archaeology Fellow and assisted in the 2004 inventory of the hidden collections of the National Museum of Afghanistan in Kabul. He is the curator of 'Afghanistan: Hidden Treasures from the National Museum, Kabul'.

Textiles from Timbuktu to Tibet

The oldest rug and textile club in the US is celebrating its 75th birthday with a unique exhibition that brings together spectacular examples of Central Asian textiles from some of the US's most prestigious private collections. Text by **Daniel Shaffer**.

1

WOVEN SPLENDOR FROM TIMBUKTU TO TIBET:

EXOTIC RUGS AND TEXTILES FROM NEW YORK COLLECTORS
11 April – 17 August 2008
New York Historical Society, New York
www.nyhistory.org

NEW YORK'S OLDEST MUSEUM, THE NEW YORK HISTORICAL SOCIETY (N-YHS), has opened its doors to an exhibition featuring rare antique carpets and textiles from the Near East, Central and Southern Asia, the Mediterranean and North Africa. Founded in 1804, the mission of the N-YHS is to document US history through the prism of New York (both the city and the state). On the face of it then, its grand galleries seem an unlikely location for 'Woven Splendor from Timbuktu to Tibet: Exotic Rugs and Textiles from New York Collectors'. However, this loan show, largely financed by private donations, celebrates the seventy-fifth anniversary of another, slightly less venerable New York institution: the Hajji Baba Club.

The US's first association of carpet and textile aficionados, the Hajji Baba Club was founded at the height of the Great Depression by Arthur Urbane Dilley – a lively merchant, educator and seeker after esoteric knowledge – together with a small cadre of gentlemen with whom he shared a passion for the art and history of antique Oriental rugs. They named their club after a likeable rogue, Hajji Baba (Pilgrim Father) of Isfahan, the hero of a nineteenth-century picaresque novel by the British diplomat and traveller James Justinian Morier.

What began as a small group of dedicated, eccentric collectors flourished, and over the years museums and institutions across the country have been enriched by donations from its members, among whom can be numbered most of the pioneering 'giants' of carpet collecting and scholarship in the US since the 1930s. Such donations, and the quest to educate, have been and still are conspicuous in the club's activities today.

'Woven Splendor' runs until mid–August 2008 in New York and will almost certainly travel to other US venues. Exhibition curator Dr Jon Thompson, a British carpet and textile expert and author, editor, lecturer and collector, recently retired as director of the May Beattie Carpet Archive at Oxford University. Thompson, who has authored a number of exhibition catalogues, books and articles on classical Oriental carpets, silk and Iranian and Central Asian tribal textiles, has also written the lavish publication that accompanies the show.

The exhibition is exceptionally broad, encompassing the diverse interests of Hajji Baba Club members as well as those of the curator, whose selection of exhibits – a mere fraction of what is available – must have seemed a near-impossible task. The show examines the rugs and textiles in terms of the purposes they served in the societies that produced them, illuminating the lives, beliefs and events that have shaped these cultures. The exhibition also looks at how Americans initially understood these woven objects, and incorporates photographs depicting Oriental rugs and their display in the homes of such families as the Tiffanys, Vanderbilts and Havemeyers in the early twentieth century.

1 | Waistband, cotton & silk embroidery, Uzbekistan, 19th century
2 | Multiple-niche prayer rug, wool pile, Xinjiang, 19th century
3 | Bridal veil, cotton & silk embroidery, Tajikistan, 18th or 19th century

2

3

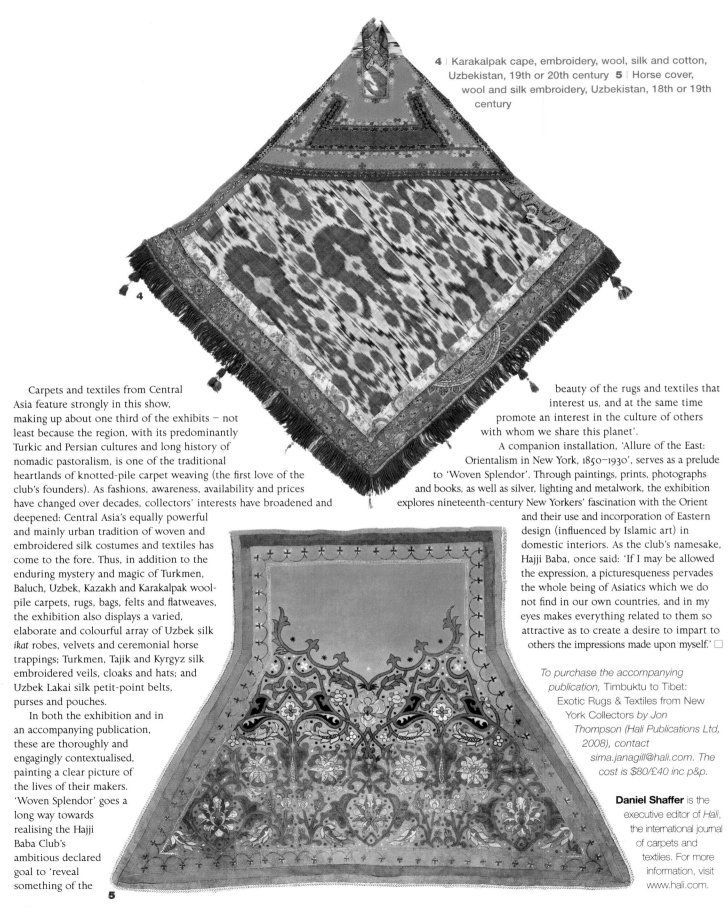

4 | Karakalpak cape, embroidery, wool, silk and cotton, Uzbekistan, 19th or 20th century **5** | Horse cover, wool and silk embroidery, Uzbekistan, 18th or 19th century

Carpets and textiles from Central Asia feature strongly in this show, making up about one third of the exhibits – not least because the region, with its predominantly Turkic and Persian cultures and long history of nomadic pastoralism, is one of the traditional heartlands of knotted-pile carpet weaving (the first love of the club's founders). As fashions, awareness, availability and prices have changed over decades, collectors' interests have broadened and deepened: Central Asia's equally powerful and mainly urban tradition of woven and embroidered silk costumes and textiles has come to the fore. Thus, in addition to the enduring mystery and magic of Turkmen, Baluch, Uzbek, Kazakh and Karakalpak wool-pile carpets, rugs, bags, felts and flatweaves, the exhibition also displays a varied, elaborate and colourful array of Uzbek silk *ikat* robes, velvets and ceremonial horse trappings; Turkmen, Tajik and Kyrgyz silk embroidered veils, cloaks and hats; and Uzbek Lakai silk petit-point belts, purses and pouches.

In both the exhibition and in an accompanying publication, these are thoroughly and engagingly contextualised, painting a clear picture of the lives of their makers. 'Woven Splendor' goes a long way towards realising the Hajji Baba Club's ambitious declared goal to 'reveal something of the beauty of the rugs and textiles that interest us, and at the same time promote an interest in the culture of others with whom we share this planet'.

A companion installation, 'Allure of the East: Orientalism in New York, 1850–1930', serves as a prelude to 'Woven Splendor'. Through paintings, prints, photographs and books, as well as silver, lighting and metalwork, the exhibition explores nineteenth-century New Yorkers' fascination with the Orient and their use and incorporation of Eastern design (influenced by Islamic art) in domestic interiors. As the club's namesake, Hajji Baba, once said: 'If I may be allowed the expression, a picturesqueness pervades the whole being of Asiatics which we do not find in our own countries, and in my eyes makes everything related to them so attractive as to create a desire to impart to others the impressions made upon myself.' □

To purchase the accompanying publication, Timbuktu to Tibet: Exotic Rugs & Textiles from New York Collectors *by Jon Thompson (Hali Publications Ltd, 2008), contact sima.janagill@hali.com. The cost is $80/£40 inc p&p.*

Daniel Shaffer *is the executive editor of* Hali, *the international journal of carpets and textiles. For more information, visit www.hali.com.*

6 | Embroidered purse, cotton and silk embroidery, Uzbekistan, 19th century 7 | Square mat, wool pile, Xinjiang, 19th century 8 | Prayer rug, wool pile, Baluch from Iran or Afghanistan, 19th century 9–10 | Two pouches, cotton and silk embroidery, Uzbekistan, 19th century

7

6

8

9

10

Exhibition Roundup

COLOURS OF THE SILK ROAD:

SUZANI EMBROIDERIES FROM
UZBEKISTAN
20 June 2008 – 4 January 2009
The Burrell Collection, Glasgow
www.glasgowmuseums.com

THIS IS A RARE CHANCE TO SEE THIS PRIZED collection of late–nineteenth century *suzani* (embroideries) from Uzbekistan. Collected as bedspreads and wall hangings by Sir William Burrell for his home at Hutton Castle, just south of Glasgow, they were donated along with the rest of his collection to the city of Glasgow in 1944 – later to become part of The Burrell Collection at Pollok Country Park.

This exhibition looks at how these exquisite embroideries were created and considers the lives of the women who made them, as well as their multicultural social context. *Suzani* represented a significant part of a girl's dowry. Traditionally, the embroidery work began at a daughter's birth and continued, with the help of family and friends, until the bride's dowry was complete. A girl was expected to have

numerous *suzani* for various functions. Examples include *bolinpush* (used to cover the bride and groom during the wedding ceremony) and *ruidzho* (a coverlet for the bridal bed).

The *suzani* in the Burrell Collection date from the late 1800s, when Russian control of Central Asia encouraged the expansion of trade and the exploitation of cotton. It was at this time that Uzbek embroidered cloths were first truly appreciated in the West. The main centres of Uzbek domestic embroidery were Bukhara, Nurata and Shahrisabz (all represented in the Burrell Collection), plus Samarkand, Tashkent and Ferghana. The majority of *suzani* are embroidered with silk thread on undyed and generally untreated cotton fabric called *buz*. The motifs on the *suzani* include symbols of health, good fortune, prosperity and fertility, and local characteristics from each of the *suzani*-producing areas are evident. For example, *suzani* from Shahrisabz tend to display bold floral motifs combined with dark foliage and the use of strong colours, while *suzani* from Bukhara usually contain a lattice design in the central field.

In addition to the *suzani*, the exhibition includes carpets from western China and Iran and textiles from Central Asia and Turkey – objects that help illustrate the exchange of artistic influences between Uzbekistan and other areas along the Silk Road. A number of events have been organised to coincide with the opening weekend of this exhibition, including a lecture on the art and music of Uzbek women and a demonstration of Uzbek music. ☐

Opposite: Cutouts of three *suzani* from the Burrell Collection, coloured silks on linen and satin, Uzbekistan and Turkey, 17th–19th centuries. The central *suzani* is an example of a 17th-century Turkish embroidery that illustrates the travel of motifs and stitching techniques along the Silk Road, as well as the similarities and differences between *suzani* and Ottoman Turkish embroideries. The two outer *suzani* are from Bukhara. Note the delicate bird in the bottom left-hand corner of the left hand *suzani*

IN PALACES AND TENTS:

THE ISLAMIC WORLD FROM CHINA TO
EUROPE
14 February – 7 September 2008
State Hermitage Museum, St Petersburg
www.hermitagemuseum.org

CONTAINING OVER 300 PIECES FROM THE Hermitage collection originating from different Islamic lands, 'In Palaces and Tents' looks at contact between the Islamic world and neighbouring cultures in Europe and China, and showcases a large number of exhibits never previously on display. The exhibition is divided into four sections: Islamic art from the seventh century to the time of the Mongol invasion; the subsequent development of Islamic art up to the sixteenth century; the sixteenth to the nineteenth centuries, featuring art from various Islamic countries; and political contacts (both diplomatic and military) between Russia and the Islamic world. Of particular interest are

sixty-nine masterpieces of Indian jewellery dating from the seventeenth and eighteenth centuries, given to the Russian monarch Ioann Antonovich by the Persian ruler Nader Shah following the latter's immensely lucrative Indian campaign.

The exhibition's star attraction, however, is a recently restored nineteenth-century silk tent from Bukhara, which was presented to Emperor Alexander III by the Emir of Bukhara in 1893. The tent has been assembled for the first time ever in its entirety in the enormous Nicholas Hall, which, even given its size, only just accommodates this majestic creation measuring over 10 x 10 m. In fact, the tent is so large that it is more properly described as a small, portable palace comprising a large inside courtyard and several rooms with a pyramid-shaped cupola over each, as well as a system of corridors.

Both the walls and roof of the tent are made of textile panels constructed either of *adras* (semi-silk), *shoi* (silk) or *bahmal* (silk

velvet) *ikats*, some of which are decorated with appliqué work and embroidery using golden thread. Descriptions of such elaborately designed and decorated tents were first recorded by Ruy González de Clavijo, a Spanish traveller to Timur's court in the early fifteenth century. In order to provide a better understanding of the grandeur and richness of the Bukharan court's lavish style, the exhibition's curators have placed figurines inside the tent dressed in traditional robes displaying examples of the art of gold embroidery (*zaminduzi* and *gulduzi*), which was very fashionable in Bukhara among high-ranking officials. Other items on display include an exquisite *iroqi* (half-cross stitched) robe from Shahrisabz and *shoi ikats* from Bukhara in a fantastic array of colours.

To accompany the exhibition, the State Hermitage Publishing House has produced an illustrated catalogue featuring reviews by leading Hermitage researchers. ☐

THE MOSCOW WORLD FINE ART FAIR

5 years лет

Manege
Moscow
28 May - 2 June 2008

Ведущая выставка изящного, ювелирного и антикварного искусства

www.moscow-faf.com

SALZBURG WORLD FINE ART FAIR

Residenz
Salzburg
8 - 17 August 2008

A leading Art, Jewellery and Antiques Fair

www.salzburg-faf.com

THE SINGAPORE FREEPORT

Books

Silver Lining

A richly illustrated book on Russian printed cloth made for export during the nineteenth and early twentieth centuries delves into the linings of Central Asian embroideries, *ikats* and *chapans*. Text by **Brigid Keenan**.

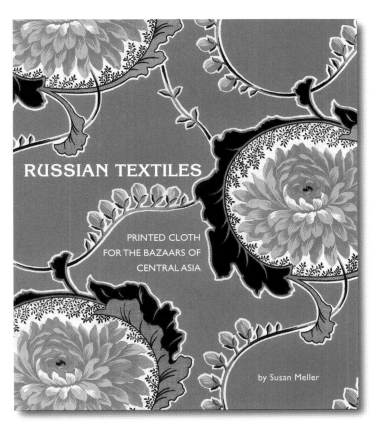

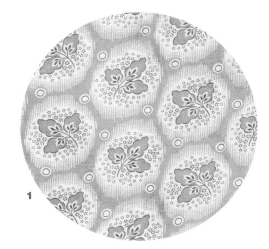

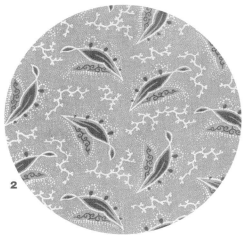

1–3 | Three samples of pre-revolutionary floral roller-printed cotton cloth, lining of a green *munisak* (a fitted *chapan* for a woman), Russia, early 20th century

RUSSIAN TEXTILES:
PRINTED CLOTH FOR THE BAZAARS OF CENTRAL ASIA
Susan Meller
Harry N. Abrams 2007
208 pp, $50

APART FROM MARVELLING AT THE BEAUTY OF the workmanship, something else is guaranteed to happen when you first look at an Uzbek or Tajik embroidery or *ikat*. As you turn it over (or, in the case of a *chapan* [coat], open it up) you will exclaim something like: 'Wow! The back is almost nicer than the front!' In the four years I lived in Central Asia, I heard this happen so often that it crossed my mind that someone should investigate the extraordinary printed cottons that line every old *ikat* coat and every embroidered hanging in the region and always elicit this surprise. I am glad I didn't try. I could never have done justice to the subject

in the way that Susan Meller has with her beautiful and spellbinding book *Russian Textiles: Printed Cloth for the Bazaars of Central Asia*.

This book is a voyage of discovery. The author lives in the US, and her journey began in New York with the purchase of an embroidered cushion cover from Uzbekistan lined in striped silk. One day she noticed another fabric peeking out from behind the silk; on further investigation she discovered a second lining in a distinctive black-and-red printed cotton that was nothing like any fabric she had seen before. This in itself was unusual, as Meller is a noted expert on printed textiles and a collector of them. She has written the definitive book on Western textile prints and is the founder of The Design Library, one of the largest documentary textile design collections in the world (it owns five million pieces of fabric).

Meller made her discovery way back in the 1970s, and has since spent time researching and

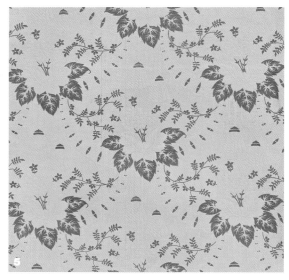

Examples of pre-revolutionary roller-printed Russian cloth (late 19th–early 20th century): **4** | Lining of a man's *khalat* (gown), Uzbekistan, showing printed stripe and floral cotton, sleeves lined with Turkey red scarves and entire robe densely machine quilted **5** | Floral cloth, lining of a silk brocade *munisak* **6** | Cloth with peacocks and roses, possibly inspired by an Indian textile, lining of a *munisak* **7** | Extremely unusual design with Arabic phrases (believed to be secular) in 6 inch discs on a Turkey red ground

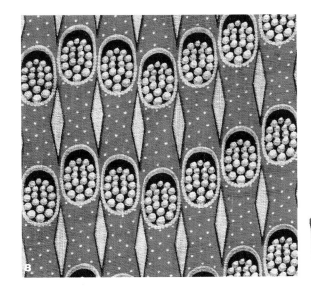

Examples of modern Russian cloth: **8** | Machine-printed cotton cloth, lining of a late–19th century *abr munisak*. This may or may not be the *munisak's* original lining. However, it has a very modern feel and is unrelated to other patterns **9** | Roller-printed cotton cloth, early 20th century, lining of a boy's silk brocade coat. Although this design may be pre-revolutionary, it has a modern look – almost like that of Op Art **10** | Design known as *TurkSib* from a series of 1930s textiles later called 'Daily Life of the Peoples of the East', in which designers tried to depict ways in which the Russians had improved the life of the Central Asian people, Krasnaya Talka Factory, Russia **11** | Art Nouveau lining of a 19th-century boy's coat, Bukhara, Uzbekistan

11

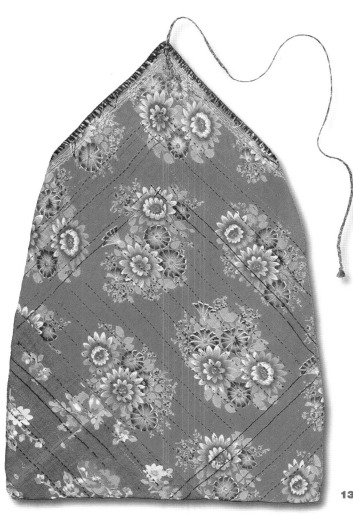

12 **13**

12 & 13 | *Turkmen bokche* (envelope-shaped bag), mid–20th century, made from recycled fabrics, including an early–19th century *chyrpy* (woman's embroidered coat) fragment lined with Russian printed cotton

collecting Russian export prints (which is what the lining of her cushion turned out to be) with a passion she ably communicates to her readers. In order to tell the story of how Russian printed cottons swamped the bazaars of Central Asia for 100 years (1860–1960), Meller uses essays written by experts on the paramount importance of textiles in Central Asia, where men, women and children all wore, essentially, the same type of robe. Status was reflected in what that robe was made of: fabulous silk *ikats* or embroideries (locally and painstakingly made) for the wealthy, or printed cottons for ordinary people.

Meller also tells us something of the social life of Central Asian people and how women stitched their clothes and household decorations together in family 'sewing bees'. Then there is the impact of religion and superstition on these clothes: as certain Islamic traditions frown on opulence, it was appropriate that even the most

lavish robes were lined in the Russian chintzes – that way the wearer would have cotton next to their body. Patchworks were favoured because it was believed that evil spirits would get tangled up in them, unable then to get through to the person inside. (Cotton linings in coats can be made up of four or five different prints.)

These essays place the Russian cottons against their unlikely Central Asian background, and this part of the book is beautifully illustrated with old photographs. (I particularly like the one of the merchant in the bazaar, dressed in a Russian chintz robe and seated in front of bales and bales of similar cloth [See STEPPE 1].) But what appeals to me most is the way Meller traces the evolution of the export prints. We see how they started as simple florals worn by Russian peasant girls, how the paisley pattern (which originated on Kashmiri shawls and grew so popular in the eighteenth century) made its impact and how Art Nouveau and Art Deco influenced the designs. We are shown how the Russian Revolution affected the prints: Constructivism inspired new abstract designs (which did not go down well in Central Asia), and 'propaganda' prints were designed to show the people of Central Asia what marvellous improvements the Soviet Union had made in

their lives. One fabric made in 1930 depicts the Turkestan-Siberian Railroad and shows a caravan of camels (the 'old, bad way') and a sleek train (the 'new, good way') emerging out of sunrays and flowers (see previous page).

Meller's book is a joyous celebration of pattern and colour, and of a way of life in Central Asia, and the Russian cottons are brilliantly photographed by Don Tuttle. Ultimately, however, as Meller writes, one cannot help feeling sad: The Russian factories are closed, and the Central Asians who once wove and wore the robes and stitched their linings in Russian chintz are mostly wearing Chinese-manufactured jeans now. □

Russian Textiles Digital, a DVD containing 203 high-resolution files of all the textile images in Susan Meller's book, is available exclusively from The Design Library. The DVD costs $500 and comes with a licence allowing royalty and permission-free use of the images. For more information, contact info@design-library.com, see www.design-library.com or call +1 845 297 1035.

Brigid Keenan *is the author of Diplomatic Baggage: The Adventures of a Trailing Spouse, published in the UK by John Murray.*

Book Reviews

William Dalrymple falls in love with *The Way of the World*, **Nick Fielding** travels *Through a Land of Extremes* and **Aleksandr Naymark** considers *After Alexander: Central Asia Before Islam*

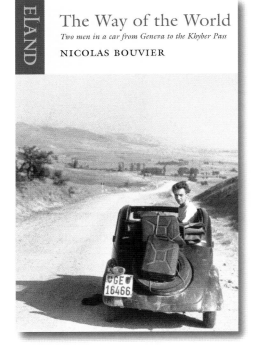

The Way of the World

Two men in a car from Geneva to the Khyber Pass

NICOLAS BOUVIER

ELAND

THE WAY OF THE WORLD
Nicolas Bouvier
Eland 2007
326 pp, £12.99

LITERARY TRAVEL WRITING, USUALLY associated with the drumbeat of hooves across some distant steppe, seems at the moment to echo instead with the slow tread of the undertaker's muffled footfall. Within the last few years Ryszard Kapuściński, Eric Newby, Norman Lewis and Wilfred Thesiger have all followed Bruce Chatwin on their last journey. Others – notably Jan Morris and Patrick Leigh Fermor – have put down their pens or busied themselves with a final bout of anthologising.

To that list must now be added the name of one more major talent, and one that I confess I had never heard of before being sent *The Way of the World* to review. Nicolas Bouvier, who died in Geneva in 1998 at the age of sixty-nine, is apparently much treasured and celebrated among connoisseurs of Swiss travel writing, but his work has only recently begun to be translated into English and is not, as yet, at all well known in the Anglophone world. Huge kudos to Robyn Marsack, his superb translator, and Barnaby Rogerson and Rose Baring of Eland, his posthumous English publishers, who together have brought this book into print in English for the first time. For in *The Way of the World* they have rediscovered and exhumed that rarest of things – a genuine masterpiece, an exhilarating, innocent, perceptive and wholly enjoyable young man's travel book, and a discovery of the Asian road that by rights deserves to occupy the same shelf as great classics of the genre such as Robert Byron's *The Road to Oxiana* or Newby's *A Short Walk in the Hindu Kush*.

Today travel writing has diverged into two very different streams. On the one hand, there are mass-market 'funnies': those authors like Dave Gorman and Pete McCarthy who have followed in the footsteps of Bill Bryson and set off in search of the absurd – and a place in the airport WH Smith – as they lug fridges around Ireland, search for everyone with the same name as themselves, take a pogo stick around the Antarctic or aim to drink in every bar in Finland. On the other hand, there are the self-consciously literary travel writers such as Colin Thubron, John Berendt, Redmond O'Hanlon, Philip Marsden, Anthony Sattin, Rory McLean or Rory Stewart who aim to reinvent the travel book for a new globalised age, in many cases cross-fertilising the genre with other literary forms such as biography, political memoir or anthropological writing; or, perhaps more interesting still, following Chatwin's lead and muddying the boundaries of fiction and non-fiction by crossing the travel book with some wilder forms of the novel.

What is interesting about Bouvier's writing is that it takes neither of these two routes. *The Way of the World* is simply a young man's journal, recording the joys and pleasures of leaving home and hitting the road for the first time. With him he brings his painter friend, Thierry Vernet (see illustrations). The artist and writer take little but their pens and brushes, their accordion ('to set the women dancing') and a battered old car. The result is strikingly intimate and immediate, as stripped down as Jack Kerouac's *On the Road*, its American near-contemporary. The two men dawdle and amble their way across Asia, stopping here and there to hold exhibitions or write articles for the local press in Belgrade, to teach English in wintery Tabriz for eight months or to help with archaeological excavations in the depths of the Hindu Kush. There is no rush: it is as if they have all the time in the world to stop and savour and experience. Apparently Bouvier took great pride, in middle age, telling people that he took longer to get to Japan than Marco Polo did seven centuries earlier.

Like the best travel writers, Bouvier has a

deeply sensuous pen. He is alert to new smells and sounds and simple pleasures: of soft white cheese and fresh cucumbers and 'the smell of *lavash* bread in fine wafers dotted with scorch marks'; of 'sipping apricot liqueur and munching nougat' in a Persian nobleman's dressing room; of the Balkan love of clear fresh water (they 'would urge you to walk five miles to reach a stream where the water was excellent'); of 'the songs and flutes of an Armenian wedding'; of a courtyard 'where a pomegranate tree and a clump of French marigolds were struggling against the first frosts' and a spring landscape 'pushing out of the earth millions of anemones and wild tulips that within a few weeks would cover the hills with their fleeting beauty'.

There is innocence here, and a deeply romantic nature, and yet there are also some remarkable insights. About the suppressed urban rabble of Persia, a full twenty-four years before the Islamic Revolution, Bouvier notes: 'Fanaticism is the last revolt of the poor, the only one they can't be denied.' He recognises the degree to which the Abrahamic scriptures retain a relevance in this Middle Eastern landscape that they can never have elsewhere. Reading a copy of the Bible lent to him during a brief jail spell in Iranian Kurdistan, he writes: 'The Old Testament especially, with its thunderous prophecies, its bitterness, its lyrical seasons, its quarrels over wells, tents and cattle, its genealogies falling like hail – all this belonged here.' He also notes how the old widows of the Middle East – 'a phalanx of Fates draped in their black shawls, silent, tough, feminine, their eyes blazing ... such sphinx-like dignity, poignant and powerful' – were 'a hundred times more beautiful than the nubile girls'.

Above all, there are some remarkable passages of prose, whose rhythms and music are beautifully conveyed in Marsack's translation. Here is Bouvier describing a Persian teahouse in winter where the poor porters gather:

They settled down at the wooden tables in a sort of rumble of well-being, steam rising from their tatters. Their ageless faces, so bare and shiny with use that they let the light through, would begin to glow like old cooking pots. They played draughts, lapping tea from saucers with long-drawn sighs, or sat round a basin of warm water and soaked their sore feet. The better off puffed away at a nargileh, and between fits of coughing sometimes recited one of those visionary stanzas for which Persia has no equal over a thousand years. The winter sun on blue walls, the fine scent of tea, the tapping of draughts on the board – everything had such a peculiar lightness that one wondered whether this bunch of horny-handed seraphim might lift off in a great

flapping of wings, bearing the tea house away.

A few pages later he evokes them breaking into 'one of those unearthly Azeri laments': 'It was as if the windowpanes had been shattered and everything that was powerful, lost and irreplaceable about Tabriz seemed to burst into the room. Eyes moistened, glasses tinkled, the song died away ... and heart warmed, one would drop back like a falling leaf into that amiable, provincial tedium, full of vague desires, which suffuses the plays of Chekhov.'

What I loved best about the book was the way it brought back memories of my own first big Asian road trips, following the route of the first Crusade to Jerusalem in 1985, then taking Marco Polo's route to Mongolia a year later. Bouvier's route overlapped with my own at many points, yet what was even more pleasurable than being reminded of forgotten places – such as the bazaars of Eastern Persia with their 'atmosphere of pillage and destruction as though Tamberlaine had just passed through' – was the sensation of recovering the raw intoxication of travel during a moment in life when time is endless and deadlines and commitments are non-existent;

when the constitution is elastic and the optimism of youth undimmed; when experience is all you hope to achieve and when the world is laid out before you like a map, ready to be explored and savoured.

Being on the road, 'deprived of one's usual setting, the customary routine stripped away like so much wrapping paper', Bouvier realises, reduces you yet makes you at the same time more 'open to curiosity, to intuition, to love at first sight'. As he writes at the end of his introduction: 'Travelling outgrows its motives. It soon proves sufficient in itself. You think you are making a trip, but soon it is making you – or unmaking you.' □

To purchase The Way of the World, visit Eland Books at www.travelbooks.co.uk. Their mission, as illustrated by this book, is to 'keep the great works of travel literature in print'.

William Dalrymple is a writer and historian and the author of numerous award-winning books. His latest book, *The Last Mughal: The Fall of a Dynasty, Delhi, 1857* (Bloomsbury, 2006), now out in paperback, won the Duff Cooper Prize for History and Biography in 2007.

AFTER ALEXANDER:
CENTRAL ASIA BEFORE ISLAM
Edited by Joe Cribb and Georgina Herrmann
Oxford University Press 2007
500 pp, £65

THIS NEW BOOK ON CENTRAL ASIA, PUT forward by the British Academy, collects papers delivered in 2004 at a very well-represented London conference of the same name.

As the editors point out, local archaeological institutions in the republics of Central Asia – rich in sites dating from the Bronze Age to Antiquity – are in drastic decay. Few archaeologists remain, and there is no adequate replacement for retired or deceased professionally trained curatorial staff in local museums across the region. Archaeologists' numbers are dwindling even amongst Russian expeditions, though these are at least partially compensated for by the arrival of Japanese and European teams. (However, this shift endangers, to some degree, the copious Russian-language data amassed during the previous century. To remind the younger generation of their predecessors, the editors have, significantly, dedicated this book to the memory of three major Russophone scholars: Boris Marshak, Boris Stavisky and Yevgeny Zeimal.)

The contents of this book are very specialised, and will be of interest primarily to scholars, researchers or aficionados of Central Asian archaeology. (One possible exception is Kasim Abdullaev's galloping overview of Central Asian monuments from the second century BC to the first century AD extending from Kyrygzstan to Turkmenistan, which, though neither complete nor analytical, may prove useful as an introduction for beginners.)

John Boardman invokes the spirit of Aurel Stein and then, drawing on his own experience, enumerates the encounters with Central Asia that only an Englishman of his generation could have had; he traces the motif of 'humanoids playing with a dragon' from its Chinese cradle to the Black Sea steppes.

Other highlights include Claude Rapin drawing on his extensive fieldwork to provide a timeline for Sogdian history; Sebastian Stride dealing persuasively with the human ecology of the Surkhan Darya Valley; Guy Lecuyot's examination of Ai Khanum, introducing the reader to the techniques and technicalities of the architectural reconstruction of an ancient urban entity (the attractive computer-simulated colour images of Ai Khanum certainly add to the book's appeal); a joint article by Pierre Leriche and Chakir Pidaev covering new material obtained during the French-Uzbek archaeological excavations in northern Bactria, yielding an unexpected and intriguing picture; and Helen Wang's pre-print summary of her magnificent book, *Money of the Silk Road*, which brilliantly demonstrates the complexity of history in the countries of the Tarim Basin before 800 AD.

Slightly problematic is Leriche's sober study of the variety of historical sources dealing with Bactrian Antiquity. Speaking of eastern Bactria, where Ai Khanum exemplifies the high standards of Hellenistic urbanism, Leriche diminishes the role of the Greeks, yet is only able to refer to a handful of sites with Hellenistic materials – he makes it sound as if these low numbers reflect low levels of urbanisation.

Elsewhere, the late Grigory Semyenov delves into an important albeit highly technical question of street layout and the size of quarters in a Sogdian city. Michael Alram meticulously explores numismatic evidence for the eastern campaign of the Sassanian King Ardashir I. Frantz Grenet, Jonathan Lee, Philippe Martinez and François Ory study the recently discovered Sassanian relief at Rag-i Bibi in northern Afghanistan, providing both an exemplary recording of a rock relief undertaken in rather strained circumstances and an all-embracing study of its iconography (although the damaged state of the monument and the poor knowledge of the historical circumstances in which the relief might have been created will invite multiple interpretations in the future).

Gennady Koshelenko adds to our knowledge of the fortification of both the Parthian and Sassanian periods in Margiana, while Vasif Gaibov adds to the many publications analysing the large complex of *bullae* found in the Parthian building of this site.

Rounding out the book are Olivier Lecomte on the Parthian and Sassanian monuments of Dehistan and Gorgan; Joe Cribb on the Central Asian numismatic tradition; Natalya Smirnova on the history of monetary circulation in Merv from the Hellenistic to the Sassanian period; Vesta Curtis on the iconography of Parthian and Sassanian coins as Zoroastrian symbolism; Alison Betts and Vadim Yagodin on the ancient oasis of Tash-k'irman; Mehdi Rahbar on the results of the excavations at Bandiyan in Iranian Khorasan; and Tigran Mkrtychev on the social context of Buddhist art in Bactria.

Altogether, this collection of articles represents an impressive cross-section of the current archaeological research on the pre-Islamic monuments of Central Asia and the bordering areas of Iran. One only wishes that representative conferences like this would take place more frequently, with their materials so well published. □

Aleksandr Naymark graduated from the Department of Archaeology and Department of Analysis of Historical Sources at Moscow University in 1982. He received a dual PhD in Central Eurasian Studies and Art History from Indiana University, Bloomington, in 2001. He has participated in thirty-one historical excavations in central Russia, the Crimea, the Northern Caucasus and Central Asia. He currently teaches art history at Hofstra University in New York and publishes on art, archaeology and the numismatics of pre-Islamic Central Asia.

THIS COLLECTION OF ARTICLES [PUT FORWARD BY THE BRITISH ACADEMY] REPRESENTS AN IMPRESSIVE CROSS-SECTION OF THE CURRENT ARCHAEOLOGICAL RESEARCH ON THE PRE-ISLAMIC MONUMENTS OF CENTRAL ASIA AND THE BORDERING AREAS OF IRAN

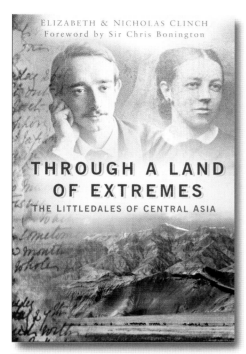

THROUGH A LAND OF EXTREMES:
THE LITTLEDALES OF CENTRAL ASIA
Elizabeth and Nicholas Clinch
Sutton (an imprint of The History Press) 2008
336 pp, £20

BRITISH EXPLORATION OF CENTRAL ASIA, the Himalayas and Tibet in the late nineteenth century, at the height of the Great Game, has long been the subject of a vast and ever-expanding body of literature. How remarkable it is, then, to discover that two of the period's greatest explorers, the Littledales, are almost unknown today.

St George and Teresa Littledale, together with their ever-faithful fox terrier, Tanny, completed three major expeditions in the 1890s that alone should have guaranteed them fame in the annals of exploration. In quick succession, they crossed the Pamirs from north to south and travelled from Baku to Beijing by way of the Taklamakan Desert before setting out in 1894–5 on their most daunting journey: a year-long attempt to reach the Tibetan capital, Lhasa, by travelling from north to south.

St George was the wealthy scion of a Liverpool cotton trading family. He was determined to travel the world to fulfil his passion for hunting, which gradually became a passion for collecting specimens. In the course of his travels, he brought back the heads of all the great Central Asian species of sheep, bear, wild camel and the rare Caucasian *auroch*. Even today, some of his specimens – many of them stored at the Natural History Museum in London – are still the finest to be found.

In Teresa, a Canadian from a prominent Ontario family, St George found a willing accomplice. She first got the travel bug in 1873 during a journey to the Middle East with her first husband, Willie Scott, a wealthy Scotsman from Melrose. Later the couple travelled to China, India, the East Indies and Japan where Teresa first met St George and spent her days with him, as Scott was ill much of the time. When Scott died on a ship travelling from Bombay to Suez in 1875, St George arranged for Scott's body to be returned to England.

Despite the fact that he was twelve years her junior, it was inevitable that he and Teresa would get together, and despite causing a few raised eyebrows in Teresa's family, they married in London in February 1877. For their honeymoon they travelled to Kashmir, Skardu and Ladakh – places difficult to reach on foot even today. So began their life of travel and adventure together.

While St George hunted, Teresa concentrated on botanical specimens and vastly enriched the collections of the Royal Botanical Gardens at Kew. For his efforts, St George was awarded the Gold Medal of the Royal Geographical Society (RGS), although his wife certainly deserved a share – even Tanny was presented with a collar that bore a silver inscription by the RGS.

The Littledales' great expeditions, as well as many of their lesser journeys, were fraught with danger. In Tibet, the couple lived at altitudes over 14,000 ft for more than six months, throughout which time Teresa suffered almost continually from dysentery. Eventually, the couple got to within forty miles of the forbidden capital before being turned back by 150 Tibetans armed with matchlocks.

Part of the reason the Littledales are obscure today is that neither of them ever wrote a book. St George completed three papers for the RGS but sought neither money nor fame in authorship. The couple was, however, widely known amongst the explorers' fraternity. The great Swedish explorer, Sven Hedin, who later became a friend, once remarked to St George in a letter that 'there is no other geographer living who has seen and experienced more of Asia than you have.'

It remains unclear whether or not St George was ever a spy during the time of the Great Game, although the book presents some intriguing clues. For a start, he had unparalleled access to parts of Central Asia that were closed to other explorers, due in part to his excellent relations with various Russian noblemen who had been deeply impressed by his prowess as a hunter of sporting trophies.

Almost as remarkable as the story of the Littledales is the story of how their exploits were rediscovered by authors Elizabeth and Nicholas Clinch – the latter himself one of America's greatest expedition leaders. The Clinches first came across the Littledales more than thirty years ago while looking for background material on the almost unknown Ulugh Muztagh peak in northern Tibet, which the Littledales had visited on their Tibet expedition. It was the start of their own passionate journey, and in this account they vividly describe the complex detective work they had to undertake to track down family papers, including some that had (barely) survived a fire and flood in the home of a collector. For rescuing two of the nineteenth century's greatest explorers from obscurity, the Clinches deserve our heartfelt thanks. □

Nick Fielding is a former *Sunday Times* journalist who has travelled extensively in Central Asia. He is editor of *Asian Textiles* magazine and has written several books including *Masterminds of Terror* (Mainstream, 2003).

ST GEORGE AND TERESA LITTLEDALE, TOGETHER WITH THEIR EVER-FAITHFUL FOX TERRIER, TANNY, COMPLETED THREE MAJOR EXPEDITIONS IN THE 1890S THAT ALONE SHOULD HAVE GUARANTEED THEM FAME IN THE ANNALS OF EXPLORATION

Fine Lines

Hafez and the Eastern Iranian World

Jila Peacock's Persian-calligraphy shape-poems are a work of art in themselves, yet they use original poems by one of the Persian-speaking world's most revered poets, Hafez, whose resonance is felt even in the remote mountains of Central Asia

WHILE ATTENDING AN INTERNATIONAL conference on 'mountain medicine' on the shores of Issyk Kul in Kyrgyzstan last year, I was asked to propose a toast at the celebratory banquet. Confident that no one would understand me, I stood and recited a short poem by the great Persian poet 'Hafez of Shiraz' in Farsi. To my astonishment there was a roar of approval from the Tajik delegation – the members of which rushed to our table, standing like a guard of honour, proud and tearful at hearing their language spoken aloud. In that extraordinary and moving moment, I understood the power of language as an *identity*.

The Persian language (which consists of three main varieties: Farsi, Dari and Tajik) is an Indo-European language spoken in Iran, Afghanistan and Tajikistan by approximately 70 million people. Historically, classical Persian was the language of the Central Asian court, although, over the centuries, Tajik has come under pressure from neighbouring Turkic languages (particularly Uzbek) and is now virtually non-existent in Turkmenistan and Uzbekistan.

Ironically, the creation of the Tajik Soviet Socialist Republic (TajSSR) in 1928 helped safeguard the language, as a substantial number of Tajik speakers from ancient Samarkand and Bukhara (cities excluded from the TajSSR) moved to the republic's capital, Dushanbe.

Since the fall of the USSR and the ensuing decades of cultural and political isolation, Tajikistan has once again begun to forge close cultural contacts with Iran and Afghanistan. Yet the old cultural bonds have never been broken, and now appear stronger than ever. Poetry is at the heart of culture, and Persian hearts everywhere melt at the sound of recitation of the great Persian metaphysical poets: Rumi, Saadi and Hafez.

Shamsedin Mohammad-e Shirazi, better known as Hafez (meaning 'one who knows the Qur'an by heart'), was born in Shiraz around 1320 and died there sixty years later. Little is known of the facts of his life during this turbulent time in Persian history. All we have from him is the *Divan-e Hafez*, a collection of 500 short love lyrics or *ghazal* – a copy of which can be found in virtually every Persian-speaking household.

These poems, which are often set to music, can be interpreted on many levels – as a celebration of love, as a eulogy to a patron or as a subtle proselytising of Persian culture and language. Yet it is to their metaphysical insight that many are attracted, resulting in Hafez being called *Lisan-ul ghaib* or 'Tongue of the Hidden'. □

Using script to make shapes, figural calligraphy is an ancient art form in which Islamic calligraphers had no rivals. Naqsh, the cursive Arabic script, was particularly suited to poetic and visual interpretation. It can bear significant distortion without sacrificing legibility as it can be read both phonetically and iconically. Based on the Arabic naqsh, the nast'aliq script developed in fifteenth-century Iran was specifically designed for writing poetry in Persian and serves as the model for Jila Peacock's calligraphic style. As Robert Hillenbrand, Professor of Islamic Art at the University of Edinburgh, says in his introduction to the book: 'When the image and the poem from which it is taken are considered together, and the reader meditates on the connection, the words of Hafez come alive in an unexpected and gripping way.'

In the two poems printed overleaf, taken from the Divan-e Hafez, the Persian text has been designed in the shape of a symbolic animal used by Hafez in the poem and set alongside a new English translation by the artist.

Jila Peacock is an Iranian-born painter and printmaker. The two illustrations featured overleaf are taken from her exquisite book of Persian-calligraphy shape-poems, *Ten Poems from Hafez*, which was exhibited at The British Museum in 2006 and is published by Sylph Editions (www.sylpheditions.com). To order copies or for more information, contact or@sylpheditions.com.

Deer

Dawn's bright awakening to my pillow called:
'Arise, your sweet Prince is come.

Drain the cup and swaying see
How your lover manifest is come.

Rejoice you lonely seeker of the scented path
For out of the wilderness the perfumed deer is come.'

Sweet tears shall soothe the burning cheeks again
And sighs comfort the cries of unrequited lovers.

The bird in my heart with glory soars afresh
Tremble poor pigeon for the falcon is come.

Take comfort in the cup and banish fear of friend or foe
For the last has fled and the first is come.

The clouds of spring look down on these troubled times
While tearful rains deliver daffodil and rose.

And hearing songs of Hafez from the nightingale
The scented zephyr, revelling, is come.'

Peacock

Until your hair falls through the fingers of the breeze,
My yearning heart lies torn apart with grief.

Black as sorcery, your magic eyes
Render this existence an illusion.

The dusky mole encircled by your curls,
Is like the ink-drop falling in the curve of J,

And wafting tresses in the perfect garden of your face,
Drop like a peacock falling into paradise.

My soul searches for the comfort of a glance,
Light as the dust arising from your path.

Unlike the dust, this earthly body stumbles,
Failing at your threshold, falling fast.

Your shadow falls across my frame,
Like the breath of Jesus over withered bones.

And those who turn to Mecca as their only haven,
Now at the knowledge of your lips tumble at the tavern door.

O precious love, the suffering of your absence and lost Hafez
Fell and fused together with the ancient pact.

Balykchy, Kyrgyzstan: A metal-framed Lenin is silhouetted on the skyline above a local apartment block

Ashgabat, Turkmenistan: Thought to be the first in Central Asia, this Lenin statue stands on a tiled plinth decorated with Turkmen carpets

Bishkek, Kyrgyzstan: Replaced by a freedom statue in 2003, Bishkek's Lenin was relocated from the main square to a smaller square

Lenin Monuments

Despite Vladimir Ilyich Lenin's request before his death that no memorial be created for him, by the 1980s there were statues of him in every city, town and village in the Soviet Union – honouring the man and symbolising socialist idealism. In addition, streets, squares, collective farms, medals, wheat hybrids and even an asteroid were named after the architect of Soviet Communism. In the USSR, a city's population governed the size of its Lenin statues, with larger areas receiving larger Lenins, while smaller towns might receive only a bust. Likewise, the great honour of creating a Lenin statue was given only to proven artists and loyal Communists.

Following the collapse of Communism, many Lenin statues were torn down, removed or destroyed in an effort to herald the openness and progress promised by a new society. In Central Asia, however, most Lenin statues were left untouched – left, instead, to the mercy of both nature and time. Although some statues have been replaced by monuments to independence and freedom (as in Tashkent, Uzbekistan and Bishkek,

Semey, Kazakhstan: This 'Soviet graveyard' was the last resting place for many monuments until their mysterious removal in 2006

Bishkek, Kyrgyzstan: Miniature busts of Lenin are still commonly found in many homes as well as on the shelves of antiques shops

Peak Lenin, Kyrgyzstan: Located on the border with Tajikistan, at 7,134 m (23,405 ft) this is the second highest peak in the Pamirs

Khojand, Tajikistan: Formerly called Leninabad, the city of Khojand is home to the largest statue of Lenin in Central Asia

Kyrgyzstan) or to national heroes, Lenin still remains the central feature of many squares – where he commonly towers from above anachronistically pointing the masses in the direction of a glorious socialist future.

In Central Asia today, many older people who grew up during the Soviet period still esteem Lenin and the ideals for which he stood. Meanwhile, there are those who feel oppressed by the still-omnipresent figure of a man they consider to have been a tyrant and a murderer. Contrast these perspectives with a younger generation that specifically seeks out Lenin to have their photographs taken at his side and those who regard Lenin statues as fine examples of Socialist Realist sculpture that should be preserved regardless of their political subcontext, and the complexities of collective history open before you. □

PHOTOGRAPHS: **CHRISTOPHER HERWIG, PAUL LOWE, MICHAEL STEEN, KURMANBEK MAKESHEV** AND **VLADIMIR PIROGOV**

Muynak, Uzbekistan: An abandoned Lenin bust in Muynak, once the main fishing port on the southern shore of the then-thriving Aral Sea

Dushanbe, Tajikistan: A full-length portrait of Vladimir Ilyich Lenin

Pushkina, Kazakhstan: A metal sign on the steppe in northwest

Snapshot

Satellite State

Satellite dishes vie for space with washing lines on the outside of apartment blocks in Turkmenistan's capital, Ashgabat. But their future is uncertain following a recent presidential decree calling for the removal of all private satellite dishes from homes in the capital. President Gurbanguly Berdymuhammedov called the dishes a blight: 'Have these dishes removed,' he said. 'They spoil the appearance of the skyline.' These words caused one commentator to point out that the dishes are 'clearly ruining the aesthetic appeal of the prefabricated concrete, uniform-looking apartment blocks'.

Satellite dishes have been a common sight across the country since the early 1990s, providing a vital link to the outside world in the wake of former President Saparmurat Niyazov's ban on foreign media outlets.

Critics and rights activists have reacted with concern, believing that the removal of the dishes will block access to independent information and foreign news. They see the order as confirmation that Berdymuhammedov is cast more in the mould of his notoriously controlling predecessor than that of a liberal, open politician. In fact, Niyazov (the self-styled 'Turkmenbashi', or 'Father of all Turkmen') also talked about a ban on satellite dishes in the Turkmen countryside, and during his presidency rumours constantly circulated to that effect, although no such ban actually took place.

It is estimated that nearly every family in Ashgabat, a city of 500,000 people, has at least one satellite TV dish. The dishes come from China and are relatively cheap to buy, costing as little as $50. The satellites give access to Russian, Turkish and Iranian channels, as well as Western networks such as CNN and BBC, and provide Turkmenistan's citizens with foreign news and entertainment shows – a welcome change from state television and its endless programmes in which Turkmens 'sing, dance and harvest all the time'.

President Berdymuhammedov has announced that in place of individual satellite dishes, each apartment block will be provided with one large satellite receiver for the use of all the residents. Again, however, critics are concerned about who will control access to programming for these 'super' dishes, and there are fears that the service will be based on a fee that many will be unable to afford. □

PHOTOGRAPH BY **CHRISTOPHER HERWIG**

HANDS FREE
Vatan, Tajikistan

Chapandaz (riders) and horses clash as they battle for possession of a headless *buz* (goat carcass) in a traditional *buzkashi* match. In the midst of a scrum, there is only one place for the *chapandaz's* whip: in his mouth. This way his hands are left free to control his horse or to hold onto the pommel of his saddle, in case he is able to reach down and grab the *buz*. The animal is killed the day before the match, beheaded and disembowelled; the carcass is then soaked in water overnight to toughen it up and increase its weight for game day

Of Goats and

Buzkashi, played avidly across Central Asia, is a game of superlatives: the most exhilarating, violent and spectacular contest to involve men and horses. **Leo Docherty** dives into the fray.

Photographs by **Christopher Herwig**

Dragons

SPECTATOR SPORT
Hissar, Tajikistan
A group of Tajik men wearing *tubyeitekas* (skullcaps) watch a
buzkashi match during *Nauruz* (Persian New Year observed
during the spring equinox) celebrations on the outskirts of
Dushanbe. The main matches of the year take place during
Nauruz throughout Central Asia, from Afghanistan (Mazar-e
Sharif, Herat and Kabul) northwards to Kazakhstan. Younger
players who are still learning the game and older men past
competition age ride in circles around the periphery

BIRD'S-EYE VIEW
Vatan, Tajikistan
Mounted spectators mill around on horseback, their saddles covered with brightly embroidered cloths. Meanwhile, other fans get bird's-eye views from amongst the branches of pollarded trees, framed by a row of Soviet apartment blocks and the rich hues of the Hissar Mountains coming into bloom beyond

A kind of Central Asian polo, *buzkashi* is played on horseback between two teams of riders competing to win possession of a headless goat, calf or sheep carcass (the *buz*), which is then carried and thrown across the opposition's goal line. Known in Tajikistan and Afghanistan as *buzkashi* (goat grabbing), the sport is referred to as *kokpar* or *ulak tartysh* in Kazkhstan, Kyrgyzstan and Uzbekistan. While the name varies, the game is essentially the same across the region, where it is enjoyed throughout the spring and summer (except in Afghanistan where it is a winter game). The largest matches are held during *Nauruz* (Persian New Year) celebrations in late March.

A match begins with *chapandaz* (riders) competing in a ferocious mêlée – like a rugby scrum on horseback – to grab the *buz*. The animal is normally slaughtered the night before the match and soaked in water to increase its weight. Riders form teams or play as individuals. Their use of old Soviet tank helmets and vivid Turkmen saddlecloths often gives the air of a country pantomime to the matches. While fighting to grab the *buz*, the *chapandaz* slide

at the mercy of the rise and swell of the group. For the players, a glimpse of the carcass is like a jolt of electricity spurring them on, whips locked between teeth, driving into the chaos. Younger players who are still learning and older men past competition age ride in circles on the periphery. Only the strongest and most senior riders (some of the best *chapandaz* peak only in their forties and also train as wrestlers) stand a chance of grabbing the *buz*. Increasingly, larger, heavier horses are becoming dominant, used like battering rams to break into the pack.

But strength must be paired with agility. Suddenly the mêlée will break when a *chapandaz*, galloping free and straining to clamp the carcass under his stirrup, makes for a distant flag at the opposite end of the field. The point is won by rounding the flag and returning the carcass to its starting point. The distances involved vary, and in some matches breaking clean itself constitutes a win. The chase is now on with the rest of the field in hot pursuit. Often two players will gallop side-by-side struggling in a tug-of-war, hauling different legs of the carcass and stretching it like a shirt on

[THE RIDERS'] USE OF OLD SOVIET TANK HELMETS AND VIVID TURKMEN SADDLECLOTHS OFTEN GIVES THE AIR OF A COUNTRY PANTOMIME TO THE MATCHES

across the shoulders of their mounts, clinging to the high wooden pommels of traditional wood-framed saddles. Block-heeled leather boots thrust deep into short stirrups keep the riders anchored, allowing them great agility as they stretch over their horses' backs. Once in possession of the *buz*, a *chapandaz* attempts to gallop away from the other players. But it is never a clean fight, and the mêlée can last from just a few seconds to up to half an hour. The horses (all stallions of seven years old or more) become frenzied and froth blood, their mouths cut and brutally wrenched by the reins. Like mediaeval warhorses, they bite, kick and rear in the struggle to get nearer the *buz* buried deep among the players. Horses and men alike fall and roll. Whips are used with abandon. Great palls of steam rise from sweat-drenched horses, and in the summer, dust billows upwards, stinging the eyes. The players swirl around the *buz* like the currents of a whirlpool, maybe a dozen horses, maybe forty or fifty, sometimes a hundred or more, often

a washing line. A truly first-class *chapandaz* can hold the calf (which might weigh up to forty kilos), whip his horse and deflect opponents, all while galloping at full tilt and swaying pendulously to maintain balance. Boundaries are not fixed, and the chase may career in any direction. Crowds of shrieking spectators scatter before the horses while the slower ones, if unlucky, tumble between the horses' hooves.

It is during this free running that *buzkashi* most magnificently reflects the ancient nomadic traditions that gave rise to the game. *Buzkashi* probably originated on the steppes of Central Asia in the thirteenth century as a means of honing defensive skills used to protect livestock against Genghis Khan's mounted raids from the Mongol lands to the north. Indeed, the very survival of nomadic communities depended on speed and agility on horseback. *Buzkashi* was a means of enhancing crucial equestrian skills and promoting the ideal of a heroic partnership between man and horse. Today,

opposite top: SUN-DAPPLED GREY
Vatan, Tajikistan
Bright sunbeams illuminate the players as they hasten, determined and passionate, towards the scene of action. *Buzkashi* is an extreme sport that can often become violent, with players (and horses) jostling, jarring, whipping and kicking each other as they battle to gain control of the *buz*. Accidents involving both horses and riders are common, and both human and equine fatalities during play have been recorded

opposite bottom: STRETCHING THE LIMITS
Vatan, Tajikistan
Buzkashi requires great agility. Here, a *chapandaz* leans across his saddle, feet still tucked firmly into his stirrups, as he attempts to grab the *buz* from a neighbouring rider whilst on the move. The horse, too, must be highly agile: able to stop dead, allow its rider to manoeuvre in the saddle and then immediately take off at a gallop from a standing start

left: TANKED UP
Hissar, Tajikistan
Classic Soviet tank helmets and thickly padded *chapans* (traditional coats) serve as necessary accoutrements for the *chapandaz* to protect against blows from fellow players and horses alike. While *buzkashi* is extremely rough and ferocious, the exhilaration and adrenalin keep players taking part in the game well into old age. In addition, riders wear block-heeled leather boots, weathered with mutton fat, that allow them to use their short stirrups with greater control

OFTEN TWO PLAYERS WILL GALLOP SIDE-BY-SIDE STRUGGLING IN A TUG-OF-WAR, HAULING DIFFERENT LEGS OF THE CARCASS AND STRETCHING IT LIKE A SHIRT ON A WASHING LINE

the game keeps these skills alive and connects communities to their nomadic cultural heritage in which, as in the great Turkic *dastans* (epic poems) such as *Alpamysh* and *Korroglou*, horses are heroic figures. In one of the earliest printed versions of *Alpamysh*, *buzkashi* is referred to as *kok boru* (blue-white wolf) – a term used by the Pamir Kyrgyz now settled in the Lake Van region of eastern Turkey, suggesting their ancestors played using this animal, which was also a symbol of the early Turkish khanates of Central Asia.

Today, the heroic ideal and a reputation for success are still sought after by *chapandaz* and horse owners alike. Stable owners tend to be traditional landowners, businessmen or politicians who can afford the considerable investment involved in purchasing and maintaining horses and providing prizes for matches; good horses can cost thousands of dollars. It is an expensive folly: as a stable owner in Afghanistan said, 'It's daft and expensive, but it's our national game.' The self-aggrandisement inherent in lavish expense, however, makes it worthwhile.

Having rounded the flag at the far end of the field, the pack of chasing horses returns. The *chapandaz* who manages to place the carcass back at its starting point (often marked by a chalk circle) collects a prize, and the match soon resumes. Prizes become increasingly valuable during the match (which can last up to three hours) and might vary from a $20 bill to a television or even a four-wheel-drive jeep. The player, not the owner of the horse, keeps the prize, but it is the reputation as a winning *chapandaz* and the respect of the community that matters more. But just as a *chapandaz* wins respect, so does his horse. Indeed, the horse is often said to be as important as its rider. In the words of one Tajik *chapandaz*, 'They are not horses, you know, they are dragons.' ☐

Leo Docherty is a travel writer. He is currently writing about his journey on horse, bicycle and foot from Istanbul to Kabul, to be published by Faber & Faber in 2009. His first book, *Desert of Death: A Soldier's Journey from Iraq to Afghanistan* was published by Faber & Faber in 2007.

opposite top: NO BOUNDARIES
Vatan, Tajikistan
Unlike 'organised' sports, *buzkashi* has no boundaries, and riders often stampede wildly off the field and into the watching crowd – making *buzkashi* as much a sport for spectators as for the riders themselves. In Kabul, the game has been known to cross busy lanes of traffic as participants ride in hot pursuit of the *buz* (seen here). Nor is the game confined to any definite length of time. Matches, in some instances, can last for hours on end

opposite bottom: MEDIAEVAL WARFARE
Vatan, Tajikistan
Evoking images of mediaeval warfare, the chaos implicit in *buzkashi* is part of its attraction. Horses are trained specially for the game, and good horses can exchange hands for tens of thousands of dollars. Today, *buzkashi* continues the long-standing tradition of horsemanship among the formerly nomadic peoples of Central Asia and promotes the ideal of the heroic partnership that exists between man and horse

above: PRIZE GIVING

Vatan, Tajikistan

The *chapandaz* who is successful in taking control of the *buz* is declared the victor. Variations on winning the game can include carrying the *buz* around a predetermined flag and returning it to the match's starting point, throwing the *buz* into the opposing goal or taking off from the crowd with the *buz* in possession. Prizes are distributed throughout the match and can vary from money to televisions, videos, camels, carpets and – when the stakes are high – even 4x4s. Such prizes are highly valued, although the esteem in which a winning *chapandaz* is held in his community is more valuable still

opposite top: BAND ON THE RUN

Vatan, Tajikistan

Fans playing the *qoshnai* (paired single-reed pipe like a clarinet), *dayra* (stretched-goatskin frame drum) and *karnai* (8-ft long horn) watch from the back of a truck and cheer on the enthusiastic crowd. The instruments tend to be played together in the Persian *maqam* style, which characterises much of the traditional music in Central Asia. The *karnai* are ear-splittingly loud

opposite bottom: FAMILY DAY OUT

Vatan, Tajikistan

Except for Afghanistan, where watching *buzkashi* is a purely male preserve, the major tournaments are occasions for all family members to enjoy themselves. At matches held during *Nauruz*, women cook large dishes of *plov* (pilaf) and *sumalak* (a sweet dish made using wheat germ) amongst other delicacies, which they prepare while singing traditional *Nauruz* songs

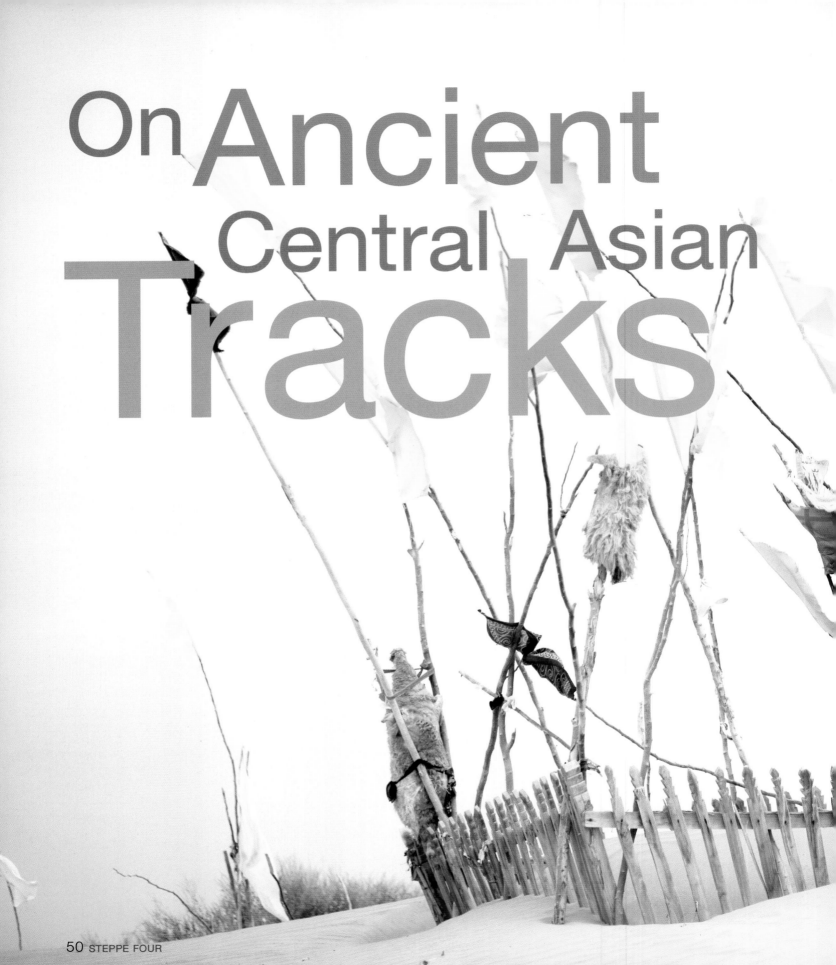

On Ancient Central Asian Tracks

Setting off with only the travelogue of an eighteenth-century Sufi mystic and a book on the Muslim shrines of Xinjiang, historian **Alexandre Papas** and photographer **Lisa Ross** observe the 'cult of saints' as they follow along the holy paths of the Taklamakan Desert.

Photographs and captions by **Lisa Ross**

previous spread: MAZARS

In Arabic, *mazar* literally means 'place of visitation'; in Xinjiang, a *mazar* is a holy place where Muslim saints, Sufi poets, mystical healers, martyrs and leaders have been buried. Some *mazars* are shrines located at sites where a saint may have stopped to pray or rest, or where a hero died or disappeared. Others incorporate elements of nature (such as trees or natural springs) that are believed to have mystical abilities to heal the spirit or body. The Taklamakan Desert is littered with *mazars* such as the one shown on the previous pages, to which Uighurs have made pilgrimages for over ten centuries

above: CULT OF SAINTS

The Uighur practice of visiting the tombs of saints speaks to a rich and diverse past and has been a central aspect of Islam in this region for centuries. The symbols and goods brought by pilgrims to such holy places indicate various religious influences from Buddhism, Manichaeism and Turkic-Mongol shamanism. Aspects of these different religions have been incorporated into Uighur Islam's *mazar* practice, also referred to as the 'cult of saints'. Colourful from a distance, this *mazar* is decorated with shamanic dolls, bits of clothing, mirrors and rocks all left behind from previous pilgrimages – each item representing faith and desire for healing and for clear communion with God. Pilgrims have their own ways of showing respect when they arrive at a *mazar*; the man pictured sang verses from the Qur'an and circled the site three times

Muhammad Zalili, an eighteenth-century Sufi mystic and poet, was not quite forty when he decided to leave his hometown, Yarkand, near the Taklamakan Desert (in present-day Xinjiang, western China) on a spiritual odyssey. He had spent his life acquiring an extensive knowledge of the classical Islamic sciences, and had become a renowned scholar in this field. He left his town for the ancient desert tracks to see what they could teach him, sure that visiting *mazars* (holy places) would teach him more than he could ever learn at the mosque or *madrasa* (religious school); he hoped they would lead him to a deeper understanding of his own faith.

Zalili travelled eastwards, visiting and venerating dozens of saints buried at *mazars* beneath the desert dunes. (*Mazar* translates from Arabic as 'place of visitation'; in Xinjiang and much of Central Asia, a *mazar* connotes a saint's sacred burial place.) Zalili slept alone by the graves, stayed with strangers in Sufi lodges and prayed with any and every pilgrim he met along his way. On his quest he met mystics, healers, madmen and ordinary people. He also encountered deceased saints who appeared in dreams or during trances, and others who made him sing and dance to show his piety. It was through these experiences, which forever marked and fully transformed him, that Zalili learned the true meaning of divine love and peace. When he returned to Yarkand several years later, he wrote the *Safar-nama*, a narrative of his initiatory journey in Turkic verse.

Yarkand, where Zalili's journey began, is situated between Kashgar and Khotan at the western extreme of the Taklamakan. It has long been a strategic stop on the region's historic trade routes, which lead here after passing through the Tian Shan, Kunlun and Pamir Mountains. The region as a whole, populated mainly by Uighurs, is a land of geographical extremes, with the Pamirs to the west numbering amongst the world's highest mountains, while Turfan, on the northern rim of the Taklamakan, lies only 98 ft above sea level. Although today Xinjiang is part of China, it is culturally, historically and religiously closer to the Turkic Muslim cultures of Central Asia.

On the road that leads from Yarkand southeast to Khotan, the wind blows lightly in early summer, while dust and the sounds of cities cover the silence of the nearby desert where Uighurs bury their saints and relatives. Trucks and buses driving across

XINJIANG HAS BEEN A HOMELAND TO SUFIS AND SAINTS SINCE THE FORMAL ARRIVAL OF ISLAM IN THE 10TH CENTURY

Xinjiang's desert roads do not venture beyond the limits of the main highway connecting the desert oases; it is too hot, too sandy and a little daunting. It is, however, along these ancient tracks, away from the main road, that Zalili and many pilgrims passed and continue to travel to seek peace for their souls at the *mazars* sheltering some of the great saints of Central Asian Islam, including missionaries, martyrs and poets.

There are several kinds of *mazars* in the region: some are monumental, bearing green or blue cupolas and forming an entire religious complex complete with a mosque and *madrasa* nearby. Others, more humble, are composed of a small mausoleum and cemetery, while many are bare, anonymous tombs scattered in the desert. But all are holy places, held to be protected by God, that generate respect and veneration – expressed by the numerous ritual objects that adorn the *mazars* and are sometimes offered as sacrifices.

As elsewhere in Central Asia, Islam in Xinjiang is deeply influenced by Sufism, the mystical tradition of the faith. A common practice in Sufism is the veneration of saints, who are considered intermediaries between humans and God. These saints are highly revered as intimate friends (*wali*) of God. Because the aim of a Sufi is to attain sanctity in order to achieve intimacy with the Divine, Sufis foster the 'cult of saints' by constructing and patronising shrines and encouraging pilgrimages. Xinjiang has been a homeland to Sufis and saints since the formal arrival of Islam in the tenth century, and the *mazars* that dot its stark landscape are proof of this longstanding tradition.

Although pilgrimage to *mazars* does not figure amongst the five religious duties in Islam, it still represents a central practice in the informal traditions of Central Asian Islam, nowhere more so than in Xinjiang. As saints are viewed as intermediaries between the

TODAY ... A NUMBER OF LARGE PILGRIMAGES STILL TAKE PLACE: THRONGS OF PEOPLE GATHER FOR WEEKS AT A TIME

here and hereafter, Uighur Muslims visit holy tombs for various purposes: to ask for assistance, to be cured from illness, to make ritual sacrifices, to pray, to experience mystical states and to find divine love; some even believe that a visit to seven different *mazars* is equivalent to the *Hajj*, or a visit to Mecca.

Likewise, pilgrimage to these holy shrines takes multiple forms: for certain *mazars* there are annual pilgrimages, while others attract visitors on a daily basis. Today, believers continue to venerate saints despite restrictions imposed by the authorities. During the holy months of Ramadan and Muharram, or during the birthday celebrations of certain saints, a number of large pilgrimages still take place; throngs of people gather for weeks at a time, often to pray and fast together but also to sing, dance and celebrate.

Admittedly, one meets fewer pilgrims today than during the eighteenth century. Though many *mazars* have existed for centuries, they remain fragile and ephemeral – not only because of the delicacy of their construction and materials but also because the cultural heritage and religious practice they represent is in danger of becoming lost. As Xinjiang officially became a part of the People's Republic of China in 1949, Uighur culture underwent forced assimilation into the Chinese mainstream through education, tourism and modernisation. Sufism, once prevalent in this region, is no longer practised openly. Some large *mazar* pilgrimages have been discontinued. Numerous changes in land use and modernisation may contribute to the end of pilgrimages and the 'cult of saints' in Xinjiang altogether, and the desert may eventually encroach upon the *mazars*. Despite these threats, devotees continue to pay homage to the saints of Islam at the remaining sacred *mazars*.

As Zalili ventured east, he arrived in Khotan – the next large trading post on the southern rim of the Taklamakan. He remained there for some time, spending his days wandering from *mazar* to *mazar*, worshipping night and day. After seven years, he left, travelling further east across the Taklamakan on a journey of several days in order to reach the remote town of Niya – home to the *mazar* that Zalili called his Mecca, which signified the completion of his spiritual journey. Upon his arrival at what was to be his final destination, he passed through eleven symbolic gates, moving from the profane to the sacred. After making his final ablutions, he arrived at the *mazar's* shrine – where, according to tradition, an eighth-century *imam* from Medina had once stopped to spread Islam in this desert region. This *qadamgah* (setting-foot-place) of an early Islamic saint is as highly venerated today as it was in the past, despite its recent conversion by the local authorities into a tourist spot – with an entry fee, explanatory signs and regulation of rituals. The sacred nature of this mausoleum, however, is not so easily converted, perhaps because, as Zalili explains in the *Safar-nama*: 'The ultimate destination of any pilgrimage is the very heart of the believer.' □

Because of the political sensitivity surrounding many of the mazars described and photographed here, specific names and locations have been consciously omitted in order to protect the sites, as well as the pilgrims who frequent them.

The author and photographer wish to thank **Rahile Dawut**, a Uighur ethnographer and author of two books on the Muslim shrines of Xinjiang that they used as guides, available at bookstores in Urumqi. Without Dawut's personal guidance and collaboration, this project would not have been possible.

Alexandre Papas is a historian of Central Asia and Islamic mysticism. He is a permanent research fellow at the Centre Nationale de la Recherche Scientifique in Paris. He has published *Soufisme et politique entre Chine, Tibet et Turkestan* (Jean Maisonneuve, Paris, 2005).

Lisa Ross is an artist and educator based in New York. Her work has been shown in the US, Europe and North Africa. To see more of her work, visit: www.lisaross.info.

ORNAMENTS

Saints are believed to be immortal and are revered with certain ornaments such as stuffed sheepskins, animal horns, wood carvings and yak tails, as well as scarves and flags – all beseeching tokens of well-being, fertility, love and spiritual guidance. Such offerings of *shidde* (wooden ornaments) and hand-sewn amulets, pictured here, commonly mark a shrine. They are tied to branches pushed into the ground by pilgrims. Each year the burial markers are renewed, rebuilt or replaced to ensure they are not lost over time

DESERT DIVERSITY

Uighur *mazars* are rich in their diversity. Although they share elements in common, each develops uniquely in relation to the landscape, history and special qualities that a particular saint is believed to possess. *Mazars* can vary from elaborately decorated structures to small mounds of dirt. This crib-like structure surrounds the tomb of a great and powerful saint. The more powerful a saint's healing powers, the more he or she is venerated. This *mazar* is decorated with flags and sheepskins as well as the body of a swan with wings outspread – a sacrifice representing great devotion. The door at the front of this *mazar* is both functional and symbolic, opened on special occasions by the *shaykh* who guards the tomb. At other times, pilgrims stand outside to offer their prayers

SIMPLICITY

This simple shrine marks the burial site of a local person. It is considered highly auspicious to be buried in close proximity to a great saint or saints. When visiting a family member's burial site, relatives will also stop at the tombs of nearby saints to offer prayers for loved ones living and dead. The *yamdaq* (broom) attached to the bottom of the tall branches is there to sweep away evil spirits

GATES OF PARADISE

The gate (pictured above) and the marker (above right) are part of the same *mazar* but serve different purposes. At this site, men and women separate; the men walk through the eleven gates marking the symbolic route to the tomb of the saint. In order to benefit from the full spiritual value of the pilgrimage, they must pass through each of these gates. It was at this *mazar* that the Sufi poet Zalili ended his pilgrimage and found his Mecca

WOMEN'S TOUCH

Women, most of whom come to this shrine to pray for fertility, have left brightly coloured scarves and pieces of clothing as markers of their prayers. Many women visit *mazars* seeking guidance in resolving marriage difficulties, for example, or to ask that a child pass his or her school exams. Uighur women are active participants in *mazar* practice; it provides an important spiritual outlet for them, as attending mosques is not always an option for women. They often take an active role not only in visiting *mazars* but also in serving as caretakers

HOLY WATER

Many *mazars* incorporate elements of nature that offer healing powers, such as a water source or a very old tree. The natural stream running beneath this wooden shelter originates from a spring on a nearby mountainside. Pilgrims come from far and wide to cleanse their bodies in this water. The shelter is covered with brightly coloured fabrics, which in themselves are signs of veneration. Inside, pilgrims stand on planks as they pour water over their bodies to bathe

HEAVENLY TREES

Pilgrims bring these *tugh-alem* – tall, thin tree trunks and long poplar branches – to the desert to mark their visits. It is common to tie flags and scraps of material to these sticks every time a new pilgrim arrives. The taller and more numerous the *tugh-alem*, the greater the saint whose tomb they mark. Ladders indicate the journey of the deceased spirit towards Heaven. The low structure visible in the distance is a *khanaqa*, a place where pilgrims carry out rituals or stay the night. It also functions as a religious classroom as well as a place for praying together over long periods of time

above and opposite: FLAGS

Sinking into the sands of the Taklamakan Desert, these handmade
wooden cribs mark the burial places of saints. *Alem* (flags) play a
large role in *mazar* practice. Pilgrims bring material or scarves to
mark a prayer or wish, and the colours of the *alem* carry a personal
significance. Uighurs believe that when the wind blows through the
alem, bad spirits flee

following spread: CRESTING THE WAVE

At this *mazar*, the sand dunes are strewn with objects reminiscent of wooden river rafts. This burial marker seems to be cresting the dunes with its sails of coloured scarves, sewn by hand onto and around the tops of tall poplar branches sunk deep into the sand

previous spread: DESERT OASIS

Poplar trees line the lanes of villages throughout Xinjiang. It is considered auspicious to be buried close to a saint's tomb so that the dead can benefit from the *baraka* (spiritual power) of that holy person; as a result, cemeteries around certain *mazars* are often quite large. At this *mazar*, wooden burial markers are painted in bright colours and maintained by relatives. The contrasting colours at this site induce a magical sacred feeling when the setting sun casts its golden light across it

above: ON THE FRINGE

Although not a burial marker for a saint, the number of flags decorating this *mazar* indicate that the person buried here is, in all likelihood, highly revered. Flags with fringes are popular amongst the Uighur and often have names or words from the Qur'an embroidered onto them

SACRIFICE

Although sacrifice is no longer performed openly in *mazar* practice, the rams' horns and skulls piled up on this wall are representative of ritual sacrifice and saint veneration

YAK TAILS

Yak tails are common ornaments used at *mazars* in southeastern Xinjiang. The use of animal skins and hides evokes the oneness of creation. Pilgrims use a variety of symbolic objects to obtain the desired benediction. For instance, one cure for marital problems involves building a miniature hearth near the tomb along with the recitation of prayers. To cure physical ailments, pilgrims leave behind related objects for the saint (e.g. a pair of shoes for problems with the feet)

HORNS

Animal horns and skulls signify the holiness of this *mazar*. These sacrificial ornaments function as offerings and markers, and demonstrate a meticulous use of natural material

HOLY RELIC

Not long ago, this site was greatly venerated. According to legend, 200 sheep would be sacrificed in one night during the annual pilgrimage to this *mazar* because of the greatness of the saint buried here. But the bare branches demonstrate that it has not been possible for pilgrims to visit this site for the last eight years. Instead, a few hundred metres down the slope, a new *mazar* has been opened. It is an official Chinese tourist site complete with entrance fees and a parking lot for tour buses. At this *mazar*, which goes by the same name, ribbons emblazoned with Chinese characters are sold to tourists to tie onto an ancient tree believed to have curative powers. The official information written for tourists tells of a Chinese legend connected to the site – a history somewhat different from the site's local Uighur history

following spread: WALK THE LINE

At certain larger *mazars*, mass pilgrimage takes place on special days – saints' days or other days of celebration. The route to the *mazar* is then festive. At the edge of the desert before the pilgrimage begins, a large bazaar is set up selling food and various goods related to the pilgrimage. Entire lambs are roasted in underground pits, served by the kilo and eaten by pilgrims relaxing beneath canopies. As seen here, Uighurs are famous for *dawaz* (tightrope walking), an art form they have practised for hundreds of years. Other forms of entertainment include magicians and wrestlers, while camels are also available for hire

ON THE EDGE

Pilgrims stop to pray on top of a sand dune overlooking a burial site.
There are numerous smaller burial sites located along the path of the
pilgrimage, at which people stop to pay their respects before
reaching the larger *mazar* of the great saint

SHEEPSKINS

In Xinjiang, sheep are a staple commodity, used for both meat and wool. In *mazar* practice, sheep are considered holy for sacrifice; their skins are sewn together and stuffed with straw, then placed atop branches at burial sites

WOODEN CRIB

This burial marker shows the care and craftsmanship common among Uighur memorials. Verses from the Qur'an are inscribed on this wooden crib in addition to a declaration (in both Arabic and Chagatai Turkic) that the man buried here lived, supposedly, to 109 years of age. The structure represents the dome of a mosque, topped with wooden crescents

PILGRIMS' PROGRESS

Pilgrims pray at the foot of a shrine along the route of their pilgrimage.
At this point, they are approximately halfway to the great tomb of one
of the most venerated saints. The camel caravan in the background
is actually an amusement ride travelling to and from the *mazar*

HOLY MAN

A mullah, and other religious men like him, line the pilgrimage route, praying. As pilgrims pass by, they make offerings of bread, candy and small change

END OF THE ROAD

Often, there are no roads leading to *mazars*. Families travel by foot, donkey, motor scooter or camel, pulling their carts over the sand. In spring, an annual festival draws thousands of pilgrims to this *mazar*. The route is celebratory, and provides an opportunity to meet different people than met in daily life. *Ashik* (lovers of God) and Sufi ascetics line the way, singing or praying. Umbrella stands are set up by merchants selling raisins, nuts and rosaries with 'Allah' written on each bead. The red gate pictured above displays writing in Chinese and Uighur that specifies policies to be observed while at the *mazar*. In Xinjiang, these are set by government officials and may affect some religious activity. To the right in the photograph is a parking area for donkey carts

following spread: THE FINAL DESTINATION

Pictured overleaf is the rear view of the *mazar* depicted here during the annual pilgrimage that takes place at this site every May. It is said that over 20,000 pilgrims visit over the month-long celebrations. This site is a thirty-minute walk through the desert from the smallest nearby village, which is where the large bazaar is set up. Often, pilgrims arrive at the *mazar* the evening before the big pilgrimage begins, and it is not uncommon for them to stay up all night, praying around the structure. This particular *mazar* contains a building, covered in flags, that houses the saint's tomb. In the background, are the mosque and *madrasa* – neither of which function at capacity today. Rooms set to the side of the courtyard offer a place to stay for pilgrims visiting the site throughout the year on more private occasions

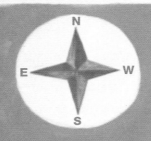

N
E
W
S

CHOLPON ATA ●

BALYKCHY ●

Steppe
Guide:
Issyk

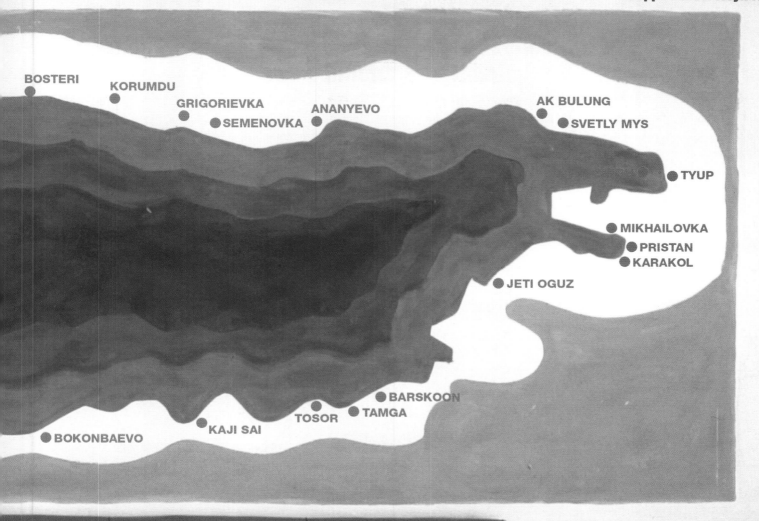

BOSTERI

KORUMDU

GRIGORIEVKA

SEMENOVKA

ANANYEVO

AK BULUNG

SVETLY MYS

TYUP

MIKHAILOVKA

PRISTAN

KARAKOL

JETI OGUZ

BARSKOON

TOSOR

TAMGA

KAJI SAI

BOKONBAEVO

Kul

This glorious Kyrgyz alpine lake and its environs offer unlimited possibilities for adventure and exploration. **Rowan Stewart** and **Susie Weldon** take us there.

Photographs by **Christoph Schütz**

Clockwise from top left: Rusting Soviet ships in Balykchy port I Road leading to the lake I A fisherman checks his nets I Waiting area at Balykchy train station I Interior of a local café I Looking out at the Lenin statue that still stands in Balykchy's main square
Opposite: Railway tracks between Bishkek and Balykchy

Set deep in the heart of the Tian Shan (Chinese: Heavenly Mountains) at 1,600 m above sea level and long cherished as the jewel of Central Asia, Issyk Kul (Kyrgyz: Warm Lake) – the world's second largest alpine lake – occupies a special place in the Kyrgyz heart. Shrouded by an air of mystery and legend, it is believed to conceal ancient submerged cities and even considered the possible burial site of the apostle St Matthew. Furthermore, according to local lore, Issyk Kul's water is believed to have curative and medicinal powers.

Just like the two mountain ranges that frame it, the snow-capped Kungey (Sunny) Ala-Too Mountains to the north and the Terskey (Shady) Ala-Too Mountains on its southern side, Issyk Kul has two faces: its northern shore heaves with sun-seeking tourists while its rustic southern shore exudes a more laid back and relaxed feeling.

Despite its elevation, the lake – with its unique combination of depth, thermal activity and mild salinity – has never been known to fully freeze and thus exerts a moderating effect on the local climate. Combine this virtue with the lake's skyblue water and sandy beaches, and it is not hard to understand why Issyk Kul is the ultimate holiday destination for Central Asian tourists. With a multitude of different activities available along its shores, the best way to experience Issyk Kul is to set off on a leisurely trip circumnavigating the lake (roughly 500 km in circumference) starting from Balykchy in the west and allowing for plenty of pit stops along the way.

As spring arrives across Central Asia, we hope this guide will inspire new adventures and relaxation alike. Hire a car and driver, jump on a bus or get out those bicycles – Issyk Kul in the summer time is the place to be!

The North Shore

Balykchy

The first town you reach arriving from Bishkek is Balykchy (Fisherman), which is also the most westerly settlement on the lake. Along the Bishkek–Balykchy road there is a monument to the nineteenth-century Russian geographer and explorer Pyotr Semyonov aka 'Tian Shansky', who once described Issyk Kul as 'a blue emerald set in a frame of silver mountains'. Further along you will also pass a newer monument to Manas – the hero of the epic poem of the Kyrgyz people and now a symbol of national identity.

In Soviet times Balykchy, a once-large industrial town whose statue of Lenin still stands resolutely in front of the town hall, was an important rail terminal and transportation hub for shipping goods across the lake as well as Kyrgyzstan's main fishing port. Wood from the forests around Karakol was transported west to Balykchy using Issyk Kul's unique wind power: the lake's two opposing windstreams, *santash* along the north coast and *ulan* along the south coast, create a rotating effect on the lake allowing for wind-powered transport. Nowadays, transport on the lake is confined to small fishing boats, sailing dinghies, pedalos and motorboats. Today Balykchy has fallen on hard times, so if you are in search of sun, sea and sand, head about an hour's drive east to Cholpon Ata, midway along the north shore, for Kyrgyzstan's well-established epicentre of beach tourism.

Cholpon Ata and Environs

The holiday haunt in Soviet times of Leonid Brezhnev and, more recently, of Boris Yeltsin, Cholpon Ata today is a magnet for sun-

This page: In and around the Avrora Sanatorium, whose entrance (below) was built to simulate the eponymous ship, which played a major role in the 1917 Revolution
Opposite: The Avrora Sanatorium – a true Soviet architectural gem

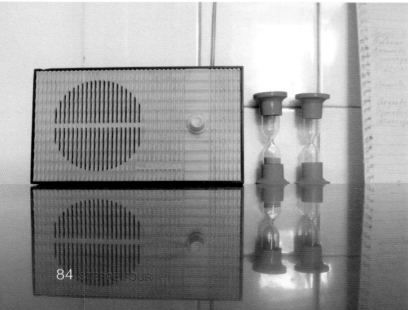

and sand-seekers and a playground for the wealthy: Kyrgyz from Bishkek and Kazakhs who make the journey down from Almaty in sleek Mercedes and Land Rovers. Stretching along the coast for several kilometres, Cholpon Ata teems with new hotels, sanatoria and holiday apartments offering a cool respite from the summer heat and a dizzying array of curative therapies, as well as water sports from their sandy beaches. Nightclubs, cafes and karaoke bars throng with life, and in summer yurt-cafes sprout up along the beach serving freshly grilled *shashlyk* (kebabs) and other fare.

STAY
Sanatoria along the North Shore
Issyk Kul's north coast was the leading convalescent centre during Soviet times, and in addition to health spas and sanatoria, Pioneer Camps (the Soviet equivalent of Scouts and Guides) also lined the shore. The lake's healing mineral waters remain hugely popular today, and resorts such as *Goluboy Issyk Kul* (+996 3943 43858) near the El Noor bazaar in Cholpon Ata, *Kyrgyz Vzmorye* (+996 3943 35648, 35649 or 35687) in Bosteri village (10 km east of Cholpon Ata) and *Avrora* (+ 996 3943 37215 or 37210) in Bulan Sogotuu (20 km east of Cholpon Ata, just west of Korumdu), offer a host of treatments from mud baths to salt caves (for respiratory ailments), massage, saunas, tennis and badminton. These sanatoria were at their height during the glory days of the USSR, when dignitaries and factory workers as well as private guests were sent for rest and recuperation in their classically kitsch interiors. In recent years, many of the sanatoria around the lake have undergone *remont* (a mix of repair and reconstruction), but it is still possible to take a nostalgic step back in time; just beware that a number of the sanatoria are in a state of dilapidation.

Guesthouses in Cholpon Ata
Private guesthouses generally offer better value for your money. Set in a pretty orchard garden, *Pensionat Regina* at 42 Gorkova (+996 3943 42823) is clean and friendly. *Guesthouse Angelina* at 21 Kurortnaya (+996 3943 42904) is welcoming and quiet, with excellent Russian cuisine. On the town's best stretch of beach, *Ala-Too Sanatorium* (+996 3942 43560 or 43973), set in its own leafy parkland, is a favourite with families and offers beach and water sports.

EAT
Cafes line the road near the El Noor bazaar in Cholpon Ata, with the most popular being *Versal* (serving Bishkek-brewed Steinbrau beer), *Oosys*, *Dvor* and *Café Green Pub*. All have a range of beers on offer.

DO AND SEE
Beaches
Cholpon Ata's small beach is littered and overcrowded. A more appealing option is the beach by the *Ala-Too Sanatorium* further west. Other beautiful stretches of beach can be found along the roadside eastwards from Cholpon Ata, at Bosteri and Korumdu, particularly by the larger hotels, although sometimes use is limited exclusively to hotel guests.

Water Sports
For those who prefer to be on the water rather than in it, the *Cruise Yacht Club* (+996 3943 43373) hires out motor and sailing boats by the hour, organises boat trips on the lake and, occasionally, ferries across to the south shore.

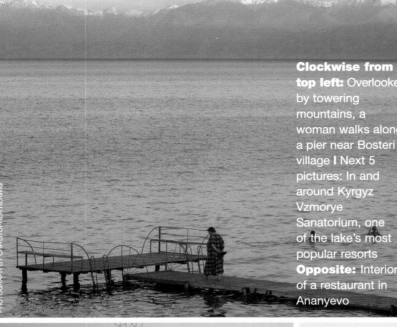

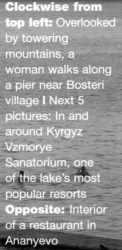

Clockwise from top left: Overlooked by towering mountains, a woman walks along a pier near Bosteri village I Next 5 pictures: In and around Kyrgyz Vzmorye Sanatorium, one of the lake's most popular resorts **Opposite:** Interior of a restaurant in Ananyevo

Museum

The *Issyk Kul Museum* at 69 Sovietskaya in Cholpon Ata is excellent and well worth a visit to see its ethnographic and archaeological displays, including local Scythian jewellery.

Trekking and Horse Riding

There are several alpine valleys on the northern side of the lake leading up into the Kungey Ala-Too Mountains. At 22 km above Grigorievka in the Chong Ak Suu valley lies a trio of alpine lakes. If you fancy trekking by horse between the Grigorievka and Semenovka gorges, contact *Pegasus Horse Trekking* in Cholpon Ata at 81 Sovietskaya (+996 3943 42450). Traditional nomadic horse games are organised annually in early August by Bishkek-based travel agency *Novinomad* (+996 312 622381).

At the far northeastern end of the lake, the wide Karkara Valley lies roughly 50 km from the shores of Issyk Kul. Used by local shepherds as *jailoo* (summer pastures), this beautiful valley is the gateway for treks into Kazakhstan, and every summer a 'shepherd's festival' is held here. Because the date varies from year to year, it is best to check with a local tour company if you are interested in attending.

Petroglyphs

Cholpon Ata's star attraction is an impressive collection of petroglyphs (rock carvings) sprawled across the lower slopes of the Kungey Ala-Too Mountains. The rock carvings, which date from around 800 BC to the first century AD, are attributed to the Saka and Usun states and depict hunting scenes, sun symbols and deer.

Ananyevo

Driving eastward from Cholpon Ata, the mountains close in on both sides and the hills become softer and more wooded. The old Cossack settlement of Ananyevo (50 km east of Cholpon Ata and 90 km from Karakol) was founded in the 1890s and has a small park and war memorial dedicated to Ananyev, one of the twenty-eight Panflov heroes who died defending Moscow from the German advance in 1941.

Svetly Mys

Continuing farther east along the lake, just past Ak Bulung (formerly Belovodsk) is Svetly Mys, a hamlet approximately 50 km from Karakol reputed to be the burial place of the apostle St Matthew. This secluded site has attracted a succession of believers, pilgrims and eight monastic communities over at least sixteen centuries. A Nestorian Christian and two Armenian monasteries are also thought to have existed here. Many of the remaining wooden village buildings are, in fact, the surviving structures of a nineteenth-century Russian Orthodox monastery founded by Tsar Alexander III in 1888, and the roads in the village are arranged to represent an Orthodox cross. *Turkestan Tour Company* (see skiing section in Karakol) operates tours to Svetly Mys.

Kurgans

Just west of Ak Bulung and the turnoff to Svetly Mys are a series of *kurgans* (burial mounds for Scythian warriors and nobles) laid out in perfectly straight lines between the mountains and Issyk Kul. A number of these large, grassy mounds dotted around the lake remain unexcavated. Excavations of similar mounds in Kazakhstan and south of the lake have revealed armour, weapons and intricate golden jewellery, including Kazakhstan's national symbol: The Golden Man.

Clockwise from this page: A swimmer leaps off a half-finished building on the beach by Avrora Sanatorium I Beach umbrella at Kaji Sai, a tiny village on the south shore known for its relaxed beach I Wooden rocket at a children's playground near Kaji Sai I Floating on the surface of a small salt lake on the south coast

PHOTOGRAPHS BY CHRISTOPHER HERWIG

PHOTOGRAPH BY TATIANA LOBANOVA

Clockwise from top left: The lush Altyn Arashan Valley, near Karakol I Dungan Mosque, Karakol I Rustic hut, Altyn Arashan Valley, with Mount Palatka in the background I Hot springs, Altyn Arashan I Flaming cliffs of Jeti Oguz Canyon, near Karakol I 19th-century merchant's house, Karakol
Opposite: Russian Orthodox church, Karakol

PHOTOGRAPH BY CHRISTOPHER HERWIG

Karakol

Karakol lies between the far eastern end of Issyk Kul and the awesome wall of the Tian Shan Mountains – that mighty citadel of ice that rears up between the former USSR and its Chinese neighbour. In Soviet times, the Tian Shan was a restricted zone, and today it remains one of the most unexplored regions in the world.

Founded in 1869 by Russian explorers, the small town of Karakol became the farthest outpost of the Russian Empire in Central Asia. Its population swelled considerably in the 1880s with Dungan people (Chinese Muslims) escaping persecution in China. Today Karakol is a convivial place, its atmosphere part frontier, part cosy market town. Unusually tall poplar trees and elegantly carved wooden merchants' houses and Slav-style cottages line the streets, and in summer their gardens are a riot of colourful flowers and succulent fruit. Horse-drawn carts are common, and herds of sheep flow through traffic like rivers of wool. Famous for the sweetness of its apples, Karakol is also the launching pad for some of Kyrgyzstan's most beautiful and accessible alpine valleys offering biking, climbing, riding, skiing and more.

STAY

Karakol gets busy in summer, so book in advance. At the top of the range, *Hotel Amir* at 78 Amanbaev/Abdrakhmanova (+996 3922 51315) is swanky and modern with comfortable en-suite rooms and a varied, if pricey, restaurant menu. At *Turkestan Yurt Camp*, 273 Toktogula (+996 3922 59896), centrally located in a large orchard, choose between comfort in a guesthouse room and economy in a yurt. For basic rooms, contact *Yak Hostel* at 10 Gagarina (+996 3922 56901), or for a traditional homestay, contact *Community-Based Tourism (CBT)* at 123 Abdrakhmanova (+ 996 3922 55000).

EAT

Eating in Karakol improves by the year. The plushest restaurant, with a range of wines and beers, is *Kench* at 225 Telmana; more central is *Fakir*, on Gorkova/Kushtobaeva, which serves a wide range of fresh, tasty foods including vegetarian and Chinese dishes. *Kalinka* on Abdrakhmanova/Koenkozova, set in a pretty, carved log cabin, has a delicious all-Russian menu. *Café Dinara* serves Dungan dishes, while *Iliusha* has good-value local food. Bright-green *Uyut* in the Jakshilik Bazaar has local food at low prices.

DO AND SEE
Beach

Karakol's only beach is about 10 km away at Mikhailovka, but it is gritty and littered and has little appeal compared to others in the environs of Issyk Kul.

Russian Orthodox Church

Built in 1895, the pretty, wooden Russian Orthodox church replaced Karakol's first Christian place of worship – a yurt. The church houses an icon of the Gentle Virgin Mary, which is said to have wept tears of blood at times of strife. Visit before 10 AM on a Sunday to be transported back to 'Old Russia' with chanting, incense and candles.

Dungan Mosque

Distinctively Chinese in appearance, the fine Dungan Mosque was built in 1910 entirely without nails and features a carved frieze of impressive workmanship. It has a wooden pagoda instead of a minaret and showcases an eclectic mix of Buddhist, folk and Islamic imagery such as shells, lotus flowers, pomegranates and a wheel of fire. Non-Muslims are occasionally allowed inside; women are asked to cover their heads.

Clockwise from top left: Pier at Ananyevo I Contemplating life on a beach, south shore I Playground at Kaji Sai I Dipping toes into the lake I Boy with telescope Opposite: Woods in the area of Orto Uruk-tu on the north coast, east of Cholpon Ata

Sunday Livestock Bazaar

Not to be missed, this thriving bazaar is your chance to be thrown into the heart of rural life as men with long, white beards and *kalpaks* (traditional Kyrgyz hats) inspect loudly complaining sheep, cattle and horses.

Museums

Heading approximately 7 km north of Karakol along the shores of the lake is the *Przhevalsky Museum* at Pristan, dedicated to the adventurous life of Nikolai Przhevalsk – Russia's pre-eminent late–nineteenth century explorer, botanist, zoologist and Great Game spy who died in Karakol in 1888. Near the lake, a massive stone monument surmounted by an eagle marks his grave.

More interesting, though, is *Karakol's Historical Museum*, located near the crossroads with Toktogula, featuring exhibits from prehistory to modern times.

Not far from Karakol, 2 km offshore from the village of Tyup, lies Chigu, considered to be the largest of a number of ancient underwater sites in the lake. Chigu is thought to have been the capital of the ancient Usun state – a nomadic tribal conglomerate that existed in the second century AD. A local schoolteacher, Kuban Imanaliev, spends much of his spare time retrieving artefacts from the lakebed, and a number of these can be seen at the museum.

Trekking and Camping

From the casual stroller to the hardened trekker, the valleys and mountains around Karakol are extremely beautiful and offer unrivalled walking, trekking and mountaineering, as well as simple day trips. Located in the mountains south of Karakol, the outstandingly beautiful Altyn Arashan (Golden Spring) Valley, alive with hot mineral springs, is the ideal spot to relax and take day or overnight walks. A ski resort in winter, the Karakol Valley

becomes a flower-strewn meadow in summer, offering stunning walks and great camping. About 25 km southwest of Karakol is the Jeti Oguz (Seven Bulls) Canyon, which owes its name to the wall of burning-red sandstone cliffs that jut out of the canyon's entrance. The canyon is one of the most picturesque trekking and camping spots around Karakol, with pine-covered hills, lush pastures and mountain streams. For logistical support to explore these areas more fully, contact the following Karakol-based tour agencies:

CBT at 123 Abdrakhmanova (+ 996 3922 55000)
Ecotrek at 112a Toktogula (+ 996 3922 51115)
Yak Tours at 10 Gagarina (+996 3922 56901)

Skiing

In winter, the slopes of Kashka Suu Valley (just off Karakol Valley) are alive with skiers and sledgers. *The Mountain Lodge*, located in the valley and known locally as 'Ski Base' (+ 996 312 531871), is renowned for its comfort and excellent cuisine and hires out good-quality equipment. Contact *Turkestan Tour Company* at 273 Toktogula (+ 996 312 511560) for details and assistance.

Mountaineering

Mountains are the very soul of Kyrgyzstan, and the Central Tian Shan has peak-baggers heading directly for Khan Tengri (Prince of Spirits). At 7,010 m, its pyramid-shaped summit is considered the perfect peak. By contrast, the highest and toughest peak, Jengish Chokosu (7,439 m and known by its Soviet name Peak Pobeda) is vast and bulky. Nearby are many lesser and some 'virgin' peaks. For logistics and assistance, contact any of the following Bishkek agencies:

Ak Sai Travel (+ 996 312 591796)
ITMC 'Tien Shan' (+ 996 312 651221)
Dostuck Trekking (+ 996 312 545455 or 427471)

Clockwise from top left: Pier at Edelweiss Sanatorium, south shore I Entrance to Edelweiss Sanatorium I Agricultural fields on the south shore I A storm brews **Opposite:** A girl crosses the road in the village of Eshperov, south shore

The South Shore

Far less developed than the north shore, Issyk Kul's relaxed and ruggedly beautiful south shore offers sublime opportunities for adventure and exploration. It boasts a varied mix of terrain, from sandy beaches and rocky coastline to lagoons and reed beds bustling with bird life, all overlooked by the lush mountain pastures and jagged peaks of the Terskey Ala-Too mountain range. The main town is Bokonbaevo, but head for the village of Tamga for the perfect jumping off place to explore the area.

Tamga

Tamga and Barskoon are twin Russian and Kyrgyz villages, respectively, that grew up around a military post in the nineteenth century. The broad sandy beach below Tamga is one of the south shore's highlights.

STAY

The unrivalled place to stay on the south shore is *Tamga Guesthouse* at 3 Ozyornaya (+ 996 3946 25338), popular among expats and tour groups and owned by *Kyrgyz Land*. The Slav-style house with a carved wooden gable has a pretty garden shaded with fruit trees and is relaxed, with a lively atmosphere.

Tamga's sanatoria gained notoriety when cosmonaut Yuri Gagarin, the first man in space, chose to enjoy a well-earned holiday at Tamga following his historic flight in 1961. If you want to follow in Gagarin's footsteps, look round *Tamga Sanatorium*, or *Edelweiss*, located just outside Tamga.

The popular but run-down beach resorts that line the lake offer another uniquely Soviet experience in tatty but charming wooden chalets set among silver birch trees. For one with its own beach, head west from Tamga and try *Hotel Legenda* (+ 996 312 662499 or +996 394 192347) at Kaji Sai (about 20 km east of Bokonbaevo).

A stay at a yurt camp offers a closer encounter with Kyrgyz tradition. *CBT's Manjilý Beach Camp* is halfway between Kaji Sai and Bokonbaevo. Book through *CBT* in Bokonbaevo at 30 Salieva (+ 996 3947 91312 or mobile +996 0503 960060). *Dostuck Trekking* (+ 996 312 545455) runs the *Ak Chiý* (Quiet Bay) *Yurt Camp* east of Tosor village, but book in advance.

EAT

Tamga's café, at the village crossroads, serves the usual *laghman* (noodles), *manti* (meat-filled dumplings) and *shashlýk* (kebabs). Head for the beach cafes west of Tamga for similar fare but in a prettier setting.

DO AND SEE
Beaches

The best beaches are on the shore between Tamga and Bokonbaevo. Packed with happy holidaymakers, they are lively and fun but lower-key than those of the north shore, with fewer discos, bars and karaoke houses. The beach closest to Tamga is generally deserted. Instead, head a few kilometres west for a long stretch of sandy beaches with cafes, including Kaji Sai's picturesque bay, and explore the lake in one of the many rowboats for hire at the *sportivnaya baza* (sports camp).

Sites

Located 6 km up the Tamga Gorge to the west of the village, Tamga Tash (Kyrgyz: Letter Stone) is an ancient rock carved with Tibetan Buddhist inscriptions. Trees around the stone are festooned with Buddhist and Islamic knotted rags, each symbolising a prayer. It is difficult to find, but the scenic walk is worth the effort.

Clockwise from top left: Lobby of Tamga Sanatorium, made famous by Yuri Gagarin | Room at Tamga Sanatorium | Treatment area at Tamga Sanatorium | Storm on the lake | Restaurant at Tamga Sanatorium
Opposite: Yurt-café on the south shore of Issyk Kul

Also nearby, between Tosor and Kaji Sai lies the Skazka (Russian: Fairytale) Valley, where the sandstone cliffs form a magical, wind-sculpted miniature canyon containing vivid rock formations ranging in colour from deep red to bright orange and yellow.

Eagle Hunting

Hunting with eagles was once a venerable tradition, but today there are only a few people who keep the tradition alive. Genuine hunting only takes place between September and March when hunters go high in the hills with their eagles and spend hours on each hunt. In the village of Jele Debe near Karakol, *Turkestan Tour Company* can arrange year-round demonstrations with well-respected hunter Tenti Jamanakov. In Bokonbaevo, local hunter Sagambay Byerkut and his family at 28 Aitmambetova (+996 3947 91320, +996 777 211880 or +996 553 404185) offer yurt stays in the hills complete with year-round demonstrations.

Handicrafts

Kyrgyz handicrafts make delightful souvenirs and are rooted in the country's nomadic past, making use of natural materials such as wool and leather. Today the brightly coloured felt *shyrdaks* (carpets), slippers and bags are enjoying a cultural renaissance, with handicraft co-operatives providing much-needed income for rural women.

In Barskoon, visit the *Ak Orgo Yurt Workshop* at 93 Lenina. In Bokonbaevo, be sure to visit *Altyn Oymok* at 69/70 Karimshakov and the *Felt Art Studio* at 8 Togolok Moldo.

If you would like to have a go at making your own handicrafts, Bishkek-based *Ecotour* (+996 312 213470, +996 502 802805 or info@ecotour.kg) offers a 'felt workshop' on the shores of Issyk Kul.

Horse Riding

If you want to feel the magic of the mountains, try the nomads' transport: the horse. The best places to start day rides and shorter treks are in Barskoon or Bokonbaevo. Longer, more challenging treks pass through *jailoo* (summer pastures) along the way to Lake Song Kul, southwest of Issyk Kul. Be warned: hard hats are generally not provided. Contact: *Shepherds Way* in Barskoon (+ 996 312 297406) or *Ecotour* in Bishkek for details and assistance.

Further Information

The ideal time to visit Issyk Kul is from May to September, when temperatures average 25-28 °C. The lake and its environs are fortunate to receive an average of about eight hours of sunshine a day, although storms can whip up suddenly and even in summer the altitude causes it to get chilly at night.

For more information on things to do and see around Issyk Kul, contact *The Celestial Mountains Tour Company* in Bishkek, which offers a wide range of tours. Email Ian Claytor, the friendly English owner, at ian@celestial.com.kg or visit www.celestial.com.kg. □

For a more detailed article on Karakol and its environs, see the feature article 'Karakol: A Russian Town in Remotest Central Asia' in STEPPE 1.

Clockwise from top left: The journey around Issyk Kul ends where it began – back in Balykchy I Pedalos on the lake I Issyk Kul from Balykchy I A calm sufrace on the lake I Boys sell dried fish and apples at the roadside **Opposite:** Old bus on the beach, Bokonbaevo

Rowan Stewart first came across Kyrgyz herder families in China while cycling the Karakoram Highway in 1993. Entranced, she visited Kyrgyzstan in 1995 and has made numerous trips there since, ultimately to research Odyssey's *Kyrgyz Republic* guide. She now enjoys introducing her young son to this remote and beautiful land.

Susie Weldon has worked as a journalist for twenty years in the UK and Hong Kong and is currently Woman's Editor of a British regional newspaper. Born in Africa, she has travelled extensively in Africa and Southeast Asia and has been exploring Kyrgyzstan since 2000.

Christoph Schütz is a Swiss photographer who has been working in Kyrgyzstan since 1997. He is the author of two beautiful small-format photography books on Kyrgyzstan: *Lake Issyk Kul – 28 Portraits and Landscapes* and *Kyrgyzstan – A Republic in Central Asia*. For orders and more information, please contact unikator@gmx.ch.

The White Ship

Perhaps no better descriptions of Issyk Kul exist than those written by Kyrgyzstan's famed novelist Chingiz Aitmatov. In his novel *The White Ship*, Aitmatov tells the story of an orphaned boy who dreams of becoming a fish so that he can join his father, whom he believes captains a ghostly white ship on Issyk Kul.

The top of the cliff they called the Watcher (Karaul Mountain) offered a view in all directions. Lying on his stomach, the boy would raise a pair of binoculars to his eyes. The powerful field binoculars had been given to his grandfather, in recognition of long service at the border. The old man disliked fiddling about with the instrument, saying: 'My own eyes will do just as well.' But his grandson loved them.

This time he had brought the binoculars and his school bag.

At first the objects he saw jumped about and trembled in the little round eyepieces, then suddenly became sharp and steady. This was the most fascinating part. The boy would hold his breath, wary of losing the focus. Then he would move the binoculars to another spot – and again, all was in motion. The boy would adjust the lenses once more.

You could see everything from here. Even the snow-capped peaks – only the sky was taller than those. They rose beyond all the other mountains, looming over all the mountains and all the earth. You could see the forested mountains that were not as tall – whose lower slopes were a riot of deciduous groves that changed into dark pine closer to the top. The Kungey Mountains too, facing the sun: nothing grew on their slopes save grass. And smaller stacks closer to the lake, which were really just bare stony ridges. The ridges descended to the valley floor, and the valley rolled into the lake. That way lay fields, orchards, villages ... Already there were yellow smudges amid the green crops: it was almost harvest time. Minute automobiles scuttled down the roads like mice, long dusty tails behind them. And farthest of all, as far as the eye could see, a dense blue curvature beyond a sandy stripe. That was Issyk-Kul – the meeting place of water and sky.

A European Chaikhana

Ben Paarmann finds a small corner of Central Asia in the heart of Berlin

**TADSHIKISCHE TEESTUBE BERLIN
(TAJIK TEAHOUSE BERLIN)**

Am Festungsgraben 1
10117 Berlin, Germany
T +49 30 204 11 12
Monday–Friday: 5 PM – midnight
Weekends: 3 PM – midnight

THE IMPRESSIVE EIGHTEENTH-CENTURY Baroque Palais am Festungsgraben lies at the heart of Berlin's historic centre. In Soviet times, this Palace was known as the 'House of German-Soviet Friendship' and was home to its namesake society. Today the palace is a cultural centre housing a theatre, galleries and, on the second floor, an authentic Tajik *chaikhana* (traditional teahouse): the Tadshikische Teestube Berlin.

Sent as a gift to the German Democratic Republic by the Tajik Soviet Socialist Republic in

the mid-1970s, the Teahouse was originally used as the Tajik Pavilion at the Leipzig Trade Fair in 1974. When the fair was re-designed in 1976, the pavilion was shipped to Berlin and re-assembled in the House of German-Soviet Friendship.

Inside, the Palais's grand Soviet-style hallway gives way to an unassuming whitewashed corridor on the second floor, but thankfully the collection of shoes on the floor near an open door suggests the Teahouse is close. One enters a splendid interior lit by candles and soft ambient light, in which beautifully carved wooden columns divide the room in two. On one side of the columns, comfortable, embroidered cushions lying on a large oriental carpet beneath elaborately carved beams invite guests to sit on the floor in authentic Central Asian style; on the other side, tables and chairs accommodate the less flexible.

Sitting with my legs crossed beneath a large

reproduction of a Central Asian miniature painting, my samovar arrived, and with it a detailed description of the Russian 'tea ceremony' from the restaurant's competent staff. The low table before me was soon filled with traditional sweets, including rum-soaked raisins and biscuits, as my tea – a mixture of strong *zavarka* (black tea concentrate) and boiling water from the samovar – was served. For the stout-hearted, shots of vodka follow.

Unlike a true Tajik *chaikhana*, you are not served a steaming *chainik* (teapot) filled with green tea; a quick glance at the menu, moreover, reveals that the Teahouse does not take you on a culinary tour of Tajikistan either. Instead, the selection of predominantly black teas is international, and the food does not seem to have changed since the fall of the Berlin Wall, when Soviet and Russian culture were synonymous. It is no surprise, then, to see that the menu is almost exclusively Russian: the *pelmeni* and *blini* are fine but not in themselves reason enough for a visit. For me, it was the sweet snacks, reminiscent of those served in Central Asia, that offered the perfect accompaniment to the tea.

Despite the heavy Russian influence, the Teahouse preserves a uniquely Central Asian feel in the heart of Berlin and makes this urban *chaikhana* a popular and atmospheric retreat. The carpets, painted miniatures and, above all, the beautifully carved wooden columns have remained unchanged since the 1970s, and continue to charm a local and international clientele – so much so that the Tajik embassy often sends its Central Asian guests here and they are always pleasantly surprised to discover a well-preserved piece of their own culture thousands of miles from home.

Until you have the opportunity to experience the atmosphere of an authentic *chaikhana* for yourself (complete with the strong smell of grilled *shashlik* [kebabs] wafting across a warm summer breeze), a visit to the Tadshikische Teestube is a worthy substitute, as well as a reminder of a time when much of Berlin was behind the Iron Curtain. □

Ben Paarmann is a founder of, and contributor to, *neweurasia* (www.neweurasia.net), one of the first blogs set up to cover Central Asian news.

PHOTOGRAPH BY PHILIPP MEUSER

Hotels

Gandamack Lodge

Leo Docherty visits the Afghan capital and discovers what turns out to be the 'ideal Afghan retreat'

GANDAMACK LODGE

Sherpur Square, next to the UNHCR HQ
Kabul, Afghanistan
T: +93 (0) 700 27 6937
www.gandamacklodge.co.uk

GREAT BRITAIN HAS RACKED UP A FAIR FEW military defeats in Afghanistan, and the Battle of Gandamack, fought just prior to the disastrous British retreat from Kabul in 1842, is one of them. Now history has come full circle, and the Brits (in this case the renowned BBC cameraman–turned–hotel owner Peter Jouvenal and his Afghan wife, Hassina) are back in Kabul.

Gandamack Lodge takes its name from, and pays ironic homage to, the English country home of Harry Flashman, the fictitious Victorian soldier, super-cad and antihero of George MacDonald Fraser's best-selling *Flashman* series. Indeed, in this secure little compound in the heart of Kabul – a city booming on the back of the current NATO presence – the spirit of empire and adventure lives on. Established by Jouvenal in 2002 after filming the fall of the Taliban, Gandamack Lodge started life in the former home of Osama Bin Laden's fourth wife. Now moved to a larger, more central compound with a pleasant garden (home to a number of docile ducks), Gandamack Lodge is an entertaining hybrid of English country home, Victorian armoury and crisis zone.

The bedrooms are wonderfully comfy, with solid dark furniture and Afghan rugs, and antique muskets adorn the walls. Double duvets and crisp linen keep guests snug during Afghanistan's freezing winters, while air conditioning provides relief in the city's blazing summers. The rooms have large desks and broadband connections, and the compound is generally quiet. Standard rooms have shared bathrooms; all others are en-suite. Room rates vary from $85 to $130.

Arriving on a sub-zero January night, I revelled in a lengthy boiling shower and settled down in the cosy dining room on an elegant cane-backed chair, warmed by a wood-burning stove. Tucking into a hearty supper of leek and potato soup and meat lasagne (properly accompanied by Heinz Tomato Ketchup in a bottle – what bliss!) and enjoying the 'Old Inns of England' placemats, pristine tablecloths and silver glinting in the soft glow of candlelight, I felt that Flashman himself might be at the next table. In fact, the other diners included bearded Americans, NGO workers and the British Ambassador gossiping jovially about President Karzai and 'capacity building'.

Gandamack Lodge, especially the bombproof Hare and Hounds drinking hole in the basement, is a magnet for Kabul's many expats, journalists and adventurers all chasing Great Game dreams. But Jouvenal's love affair with the country runs deeper. Determined to be a combat photographer, he completed a brief stint in the British army before travelling

overland to Afghanistan in 1979. The next ten years saw him make seventy-two perilous sorties to film the mujahideen fighting the Soviets. Almost thirty years later he is still here, married to the vivacious Hassina and raising a young family. Generous with his vast experience and network of contacts, Jouvenal is the ultimate Kabul fixer.

The morning after my arrival, having had a dreamy night's sleep, I flung back the curtains and was dazzled by the glistening snowbound peaks that dominate Kabul. Breakfasting in glorious sunshine on hot croissants, coffee and fresh orange juice, with a miniature moustachioed Flashman grinning at me from my teacup, I reflected that when it comes to British retreats in Afghanistan, Gandamack Lodge is a notable success. □

Harry Flashman, the legendary, nineteenth-century James Bond-style character, was first introduced to readers of the Flashman *series as a soldier in the first Anglo-Afghan War, that major Great Game conflict, which resulted in British withdrawal from Afghanistan. Throughout the series, he dazzled readers with his colourful renditions of Imperial history and racy escapades in which he unabashedly placed himself on the front line of the major wars and uproars (as well as boudoirs and harems) of the time. Ultimately, Flashman was a coward, running from the danger he constantly found himself in, yet always managing to arrive at the end of each volume with medals, high praise and the adoration of a string of beautiful women.*

With the money he made from the looting of Lucknow during the Indian Mutiny in 1858, Flashman settled in England's Leicestershire countryside and named his new home Gandamack Lodge in memory of the British defeat at Gandamack and his own lucky escape from that battle. Historically, the only man to actually survive the siege at Gandamack (during the British retreat from Kabul to Jalalabad in 1842) was Dr William Brydon. Today, in Afghanistan, Flashman's lodge lives on in true pioneering style.

Leo Docherty is a travel writer. He is currently writing about his journey on horse, bicycle and foot from Istanbul to Kabul, to be published by Faber & Faber in 2009. His first book, *Desert of Death: A Soldier's Journey from Iraq to Afghanistan*, was published by Faber & Faber in 2007.

Noodles from the Other China

Xinjiang is a noodle-eater's paradise. During their travels there over the last twenty-five years, including recent research trips for their latest book, *Beyond the Great Wall: Recipes and Travels in the Other China*, **Naomi Duguid** and **Jeffrey Alford** have eaten – and have watched people knead, shape and cook – a stupendous quantity of noodles. Photographs by **Richard Jung.**

Uighurs, numbering approximately nine million people out of a population of nearly twenty million, comprise the majority of China's Xinjiang Uighur Autonomous Region. Most live in the oases that rim the Taklamakan Desert – towns and cities such as Aksu, Korla, Kashgar, Turfan and Khotan – as well as in the capital, Urumqi. Noodles are a staple food for many of the peoples of Xinjiang. Uighurs in particular are famous throughout China and beyond for their extraordinary flung noodles. A smooth, well-kneaded wheat flour dough is shaped into a short rope, which is then taken, one end in each hand, and flung a little like a skipping rope, so that the weight of the dough stretches it longer. The thinner rope is then doubled and the flinging repeated. So it goes, until the noodle makers have many thinner strands of stretched dough in their hands. It is a fascinating process that takes practice, and although we have tried and tried, we confess that we have not yet mastered the technique.

The Uighurs have a simpler noodle, too – the most basic of all the noodles we know. Small pieces of dough are torn off, kneaded well and dropped into boiling water or broth. They look a little like gnocchi and are slightly resistant to the bite, yet tender. They make a great introduction to the world of handmade noodles. We usually top them with a version of *laghman*, the traditional Uighur sauce of tomatoes, peppers and lamb.

Xinjiang is also home to several other Muslim Turkic groups who each have their own (and sometimes easier) techniques for making noodles. Along the Kazakh border in the Altai Mountains at the northern tip of Xinjiang, we found Kazakhs and Tuvans living with their herds of horses, cattle, goats and camels. The Kazakhs there make hand-stretched noodles, while the Tuvan noodles we encountered are more like European noodles: rolled-out dough cut into strips. In both traditions the noodles are cooked in a flavoured broth or stew to make a one-dish meal – the noodle equivalent of *plov* (pilaf). We have seen Kazakh women in yurts and houses deftly hand-stretch noodles, dropping them into a boiling broth as they work. The noodles, richly flavoured by the broth, are then served on a large platter. Traditionally they are topped with meat, bones and some chopped onion, with a small bowl of broth on the side. The Kazakhs then eat the dish with their hands – those most sensual of eating implements.

KAZAKH NOODLE BROTH

So simple it may not even constitute a recipe, this broth was nevertheless new to us. In the Altai Mountains sitting on carpets and leaning against padded quilts in Kazakh yurts, we watched as meals were cooked over a small portable iron stove fuelled with wood. Often prepared just with a pressure cooker, these meals were some of the simplest and best meals we have ever eaten.

The woman of the house would have goat shank boiling to make a broth. While it was cooking, she would make noodle dough. When the broth was ready, she would release steam from the pressure cooker and take the meat out of the pot. With the broth still hot on top of the stove, she would then deftly stretch the dough strips into noodles by hand, tossing each individual noodle into the broth when stretched. Almost instantly, she had all the noodles formed and cooking. Every cook made it look incredibly easy.

When the noodles were just tender, the cook strained them from the broth, placed them onto a large platter and then sliced a raw onion on top. The large pieces of bone were placed on top with a smattering of meat; then everyone would dig in, using the right hand only. About midway through the meal, the broth would be poured into small individual soup bowls so we could drink it alongside the noodles.

Returning home from northern Xinjiang, we were determined to buy a pressure cooker. But in the end, we just bought goat shanks and cooked them in a large soup pot. It was so easy and so good.

Servings:
Makes about 8 cups soup broth plus meat and bones; serves 4–6 people as a one-dish meal with noodles, or 8 people as a clear soup

Ingredients:
1½ lbs goat shank (or lamb shank) cut into 1-in lengths
16 cups cold water
Salt

Preparation:
● Place a cast-iron or other heavy pot or pressure cooker over low heat. Add the pieces of shank and brown all over, without oil, for approximately 15 minutes.
● Add water, raise heat to bring it to a vigorous boil, then lower heat and simmer, partially covered, for 2 to 3 hours.
● Remove bones and meat and measure the volume of soup. Add 1/2 tsp of salt for every cup of soup, then taste and adjust if desired. Serve as a clear soup, or use in the traditional way to cook Kazakh Hand-Stretched Noodles (or, if you prefer, other homemade or store-bought noodles). If making noodles, serve either with the noodles in the broth or as a side soup to a platter of noodles, as you please.

KAZAKH HAND-STRETCHED NOODLES

You can make the noodles just before you want to cook them, or instead make them ahead of time and hang them to dry for as long as several days before cooking them (see Dried Kazakh Noodles opposite). It is just a matter of what is most convenient for you. The dough should be made at least 30 minutes or up to 2 hours before shaping the noodles.

Servings:
Makes about 1½ lbs long fresh egg noodles; serves 4 people as a one-dish main course or 6 people as a hearty soup course

Ingredients:
3 cups all-purpose/hard flour, plus extra for surfaces
1½ tsp salt
2 large eggs
About ¾ cup of lukewarm water

Preparation:
● At least 1 hour before you wish to serve the noodles, place the flour, salt and eggs in a food processor and process briefly. With the blades spinning, slowly pour water through the feed tube until a ball of dough forms. Turn out onto a lightly floured surface and knead briefly. Alternatively, if working by hand, place the flour, salt and eggs in a medium bowl and whisk or stir to combine them. Add 3/4 cup lukewarm water and stir to mix it in. If the mixture is still dry or stiff, mix in a little extra water. Turn out onto a lightly floured surface and knead until smooth (about 3 minutes).
● Working on a lightly floured surface, cut the dough into 4 equal pieces. Flatten each piece out to a long rectangle approximately 12 in long and 3 in wide. Use a sharp knife or a metal-edged dough scraper to cut the rectangles crosswise into strips just under 1/2 in wide. Cover the dough with a cloth or with plastic wrap, and set aside to rest for 30 minutes or for as long as 2 hours.
● Before starting to stretch the noodles, lightly dust a large surface with a little flour. You will then be able to dust the stretched noodles with flour to keep them from sticking, and you can lay them on the floured surface when they are shaped.
● Stretching the dough the Kazakh way is amazingly easy. While this paragraph may have a lot of words, once you pick up a piece of dough and feel how it yields and thins with the pressure of your fingers and thumbs, you will find your own technique. Pick up a dough strip and touch both sides of it to the floured surface. Pinch it gently near one end between thumb and forefinger, holding it nearer the centre with the thumb and index finger of your other hand. You will be stretching it both by pinching it along its length and also by pulling the pinched section gently away from where you are holding it in your other hand. Gradually work your way along the strip, pinching it and gently pulling your hands apart a little as you do. This will flatten and stretch it. When the strip is 12 to 15 in long and thinner and a little wider, touch it to the floured surface to dust it with flour. Then set it to one side on a lightly floured surface.

DRIED KAZAKH NOODLES

If you would rather make the noodles ahead of time so you do not feel rushed, then make the dough (opposite) and let it rest as follows. Before starting to shape the noodles, prepare a rack arrangement that you can hang the noodles on to dry. (We use the backs of wooden chairs or, if we are making a larger quantity, a wooden clothes rack. In China you will often see wheat flour noodles set out to dry on a clothesline or clothes racks.) Shape the first noodle, then set it briefly on the floured surface to flour it before hanging it on a dowel or rack to dry. Repeat with the remaining noodles. Let them dry for as short as 1 hour to as long as several days. Cook as directed opposite. You will find that the dried noodles take a little longer to cook (about 10 minutes in our experience), but are just as successful as the fresh ones.

SOY-VINEGAR SAUCE

This classic condiment is a great accompaniment for any noodle soup. Make it fresh just before you wish to serve it, or put out the soy sauce, vinegar and a small plate of minced spring onion, and invite guests to help themselves, adjusting the flavours as they eat.

Ingredients:

½ cup soy sauce
¼ cup aged black rice vinegar or substitute rice vinegar
About 2 tbsp minced spring onion

Preparation:

● Place in a bowl and stir together. Serve with a spoon so guests can drizzle the sauce on their noodles to taste. □

Naomi Duguid and **Jeffrey Alford** are travellers, photographers, writers and cooks. Together they have co-authored five award-winning cookbooks that explore food in a cultural context, including *Flatbreads & Flavors* [see STEPPE 3], *Seductions of Rice* and *Hot Sour Salty Sweet*. Their latest book, *Beyond the Great Wall: Recipes and Travels in the Other China* (2008), from which the recipes in this feature are taken, is published by Artisan in the US and by Random House in Canada.

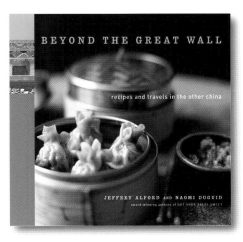

● Repeat with the remaining dough strips. We often make these with one of our children or with a guest. This way the work goes quickly, and everyone becomes well-practised at noodle stretching.
● Once all the noodles are shaped, bring a pot of at least 6 cups of broth to a vigorous boil. Add the noodles, bring back to a boil and cook as you would pasta, until tender but still firm to the bite (about 6 minutes). Use a mesh basket or tongs to lift the noodles out of the broth and onto wide individual soup plates, or else into a large bowl or onto a platter.

Products

THE HOOPOE YURT HOTEL | If Central Asia seems just that little bit too far away this summer but you still fancy spotting a hoopoe and sleeping in a nomadic tent, why not take a break at The Hoopoe Yurt Hotel in southern Spain instead? Set on three hectares of olive groves and unspoilt cork oak forest, and with spectacular views of Andalucía's Grazalema Mountains, this hotel is the perfect getaway.

Combining a back-to-nature experience with one of luxury, each of the four themed yurts (Afghan [shown above], Mongolian, Jaipur and Safari) has a double bed, private bathroom complete with piping hot showers, eco-loos and solar-powered electricity. The yurts are set on an acre of their own private meadow with hammocks and comfortable shaded seating areas outside. Guests are treated to delicious continental breakfasts, and four nights a week it is possible to dine at the hotel on the freshest of local food.

There is plenty to do and see in this region of southern Spain, including visits to nearby historical sites and thriving local towns, plus riding, walking, birdwatching, visiting local sherry bodegas and taking trips to the coast.
The hotel is open for the 2008 season from April until mid-October, and a yurt (with double bed) costs £95 per night with breakfast for two. For more information, visit www.yurthotel.com.

LONELY PLANET AFGHANISTAN | Around thirty-five years ago, Afghanistan was one of the main destinations on the 'hippy trail' and a mecca for backpackers and other travellers who went to soak up the country's rich, timeless and laid-back culture. Given its recent history, however, backpackers are few and far between. Instead, the new *Lonely Planet Afghanistan* guide is, by its own admission, aimed at expats and aid workers moving to the country and provides 'practical tips as well as useful content'. Introducing boxed texts labelled 'Risk Assessment' at the beginning of every chapter, the guide makes clear the hazards of travelling in Afghanistan. However, it simultaneously highlights some of the more beautiful aspects of the country's history and culture; it is only sad that so many of those attractions cannot be shared by the Afghan people – at least for the time being.
Lonely Planet Afghanistan by Paul Clammer, Lonely Planet Publications (£15.99/$25.99)

LONELY PLANET CENTRAL ASIA | The revised edition of *Lonely Planet Central Asia* is a slimmed-down version of the previous two editions and covers the five post-Soviet Central Asian states. Significant additions include an updated section on Kazakhstan's ever-growing capital, Astana, and new information on the quick turnover of hotels and restaurants in the region. It also brings with it a more upbeat approach to the region as a whole, recognising perhaps that Central Asia, unspoilt by mass tourism, is a region of immense hospitality and inspiring natural beauty.
Lonely Planet Central Asia by Bradley Mayhew, Greg Bloom, John Noble and Dean Starnes, Lonely Planet Publications (£17.99/$29.99)

THE DESIGN LIBRARY | With the world's largest and best organised collection of documentary fabrics, wallpapers, embroideries, original paintings and yarn dyes, it is no wonder that *The New York Times* described the Design Library (New York office pictured right) as akin to '… being let loose unsupervised in the archives of the Victoria and Albert Museum.' Its core business is the sale and licensing of antique, vintage, contemporary and modern textile designs to the fashion, home furnishings, textile and paper product industries, amongst others. The textile collection dates from the 1750s to the late twentieth century and numbers some five million designs sorted into 900 categories. Included in the vast and diverse archives is a collection of nineteenth- and twentieth-century Central Asian textiles – *suzani*, *ikats*, robes, skullcaps, etc, including Russian printed cottons – the likes of which are highlighted in this issue's feature book review on page 21.
For more information and to get in touch, visit www.design-library.com. □

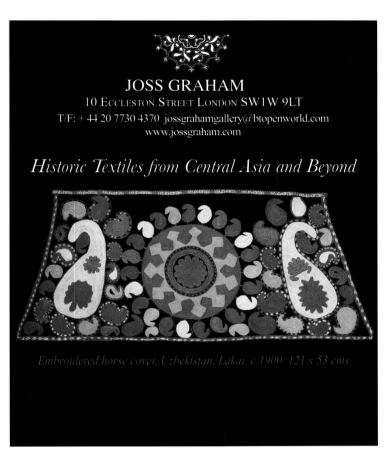

Snapshot

Boomtown Birthday

The best views of Kazakhstan's capital, Astana, are had from Baiterek (Kazakh: Tree of Life), a spherical observation tower nearly 100 m tall symbolising a Kazakh legend in which a mythical bird lays a golden egg in a poplar tree. From this vantage point, the scale of Astana's construction is clearly visible: cranes and skyscrapers rise in all directions, in stark contrast with the vast emptiness of the surrounding steppe.

As fast money is made from the country's natural resources, new buildings rise up seemingly overnight. Over the last five years, Kazakhstan's economy has grown by an average of 9–10 percent annually thanks to its vast oil and mineral wealth. The construction industry alone has grown over 20 percent per annum.

In 1997, President Nazarbayev embarked on one of his grandest projects yet – the construction of a brand new capital city in the middle of the steppe – when the Kazakh government relocated from Almaty to Astana. The new capital was officially unveiled in 1998; Astana has since become one of the world's largest building projects, with a price tag of at least $15 billion so far – part of a monumental campaign to establish itself as a hub, not only in Central Asia, but also internationally. The construction boom has attracted firms from all over the world. Local Kazakh construction companies compete for bids alongside those from Turkey, Switzerland, Italy, Kuwait and Jordan. Once a Russian military outpost and then home to one of Stalin's most notorious Gulags, Astana now attracts star architects such as Britain's Norman Foster and Italy's Manfredi Nicoletti.

This July, Astana will celebrate its tenth anniversary. Grand plans are under way with over forty major events scheduled, including the unveiling of new bridges and parks and the commissioning of new cultural, healthcare and sports facilities. Over 100 international delegations have been invited to take part, and reports suggest that talks with Sir Paul McCartney, Pink Floyd and even Jennifer Lopez have taken place. It will be one party on the steppe that ought not to be missed. □

This photograph was developed using a technique called cross-processing, in which slide film is deliberately processed in a chemical solution intended for a different type of film. The result is a negative image characterised by unnatural colours and high contrast on a colourless base.

PHOTOGRAPH BY **PHILIPP JAHN**

Classifieds

From *The Nomads in Anatolia*, by Harald Böhmer, featured in CORNUCOPIA 39

CORNUCOPIA
THE MAGAZINE FOR CONNOISSEURS OF TURKEY
www.cornucopia.net

Central Asian Arts Association

Promoting and marketing art of Central Asia
www.central-asian-arts.com

IDP
THE SILK ROAD ONLINE

A Central Asian treasure-trove of
- manuscripts & artefacts
- historical photographs
- expedition accounts
- archaeological site plans
- maps and more...

  all freely available online.

http://idp.bl.uk
International Dunhuang Project
The British Library,
96 Euston Road,
London NW1 2DB, UK

cocoon

Arasta Bazaar No: 93, 34122 Sultanahmet
Istanbul, cocoon@cocoontr.com
cell: + 90 (0533)7606792, tel: +90 (0212) 5180338,
www.cocoontr.com

SALOR MAIN RUG FRAGMENT, 18TH CENTURY

shish®

Serving the freshest & tastiest menu, this side of the Silk Road

71-75 Bishops Bridge Road, W2   T:020 7229 7300
313-319 Old Street, EC1V   T:020 7749 0990
2-6 Station Parade, Willesden Green, NW2
T:020 8208 9292
www.shish.com

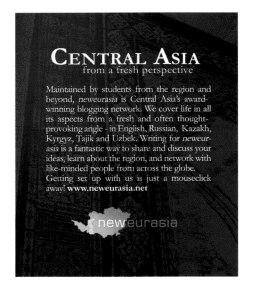

CENTRAL ASIA
from a fresh perspective

Maintained by students from the region and beyond, *neweurasia* is Central Asia's award-winning blogging network. We cover life in all its aspects from a fresh and often thought-provoking angle - in English, Russian, Kazakh, Kyrgyz, Tajik and Uzbek. Writing for *neweurasia* is a fantastic way to share and discuss your ideas, learn about the region, and network with like-minded people from across the globe. Getting set up with us is just a mouseclick away! www.neweurasia.net

neweurasia

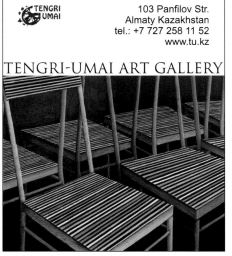

TENGRI UMAI

103 Panfilov Str.
Almaty Kazakhstan
tel.: +7 727 258 11 52
www.tu.kz

TENGRI-UMAI ART GALLERY

TRAVEL AGENCY
LEGENDES DE SAMARCANDE M7
UZBEKISTAN

parle français

B&B LEGENDE
old town SAMARKAND
60, Tolmasova Street

T: +998/662-33 74 81
35 05 43
F: +998/662-31 20 13
legendm7@rol.uz
www.legendm7.intal.uz

Double Take in Kashgar

Khalid Abdalla, who starred in the film *The Kite Runner* as the grown-up Amir, talks about preparing for his role in Afghanistan and filming on location in western China

WHEN IT WAS ANNOUNCED THAT KHALED HOSSEINI'S BEST-selling novel *The Kite Runner* was being turned into a film, the concern of those who had fallen in love with the book was also shared by many of us given the task of trying to adapt if for the screen. I often heard claims from makeup artists, electricians, actors and the script supervisor that this was one of their favourite books and that they had jumped at the opportunity to work on the film. Therefore, the pressure to get it right was not only well understood but also self-imposed.

Knowing that Marc Forster, our director, wanted to keep a realistic handle on the world of the book by shooting the film partially in Dari, I felt secure that we were being helmed by someone who wanted to follow the book's lead and keep it culturally alive. Perhaps most important was the decision to cast, as much as possible, in Afghanistan and the region, allowing a wealth of 'lived' experience to find its way into the film. For me, a British-born Egyptian brought up speaking English and Arabic, it meant travelling to Afghanistan and immersing myself in its language and culture.

With only six days' notice, I arrived in Kabul and spent one month in Afghanistan, during which time I had between four and five hours of Dari lessons every day. I became well acquainted with Kabul and also travelled to Bamiyan in the west and through the Salang Pass to Mazar-e Sharif. Together with my teacher, Sattar, I took a double-pronged approach of working on the Dari dialogue in the script, in addition to regular language lessons. These initiatives started out as independent pursuits but ended up helping each other tremendously; the words I was learning phonetically in the script began to make sense to me whilst simultaneously bolstering the range of my vocabulary. Outside lessons, I spent time with my driver, Ali Khan, and insisted on speaking Dari with him at every opportunity. Together with Ali Khan and with my Arabic (Dari has many Arabic loanwords), by the time I left Kabul I had started to confuse Afghans as to my origins.

For obvious reasons, the Afghan scenes in the film were not shot in Afghanistan. Instead, they were filmed in Kashgar and Tashkorgan in Xinjiang. The location managers were looking for somewhere that could double as Afghanistan in the 1970s and as Afghanistan under Taliban control. They scouted locations in Turkey, Morocco and India but finally chose Xinjiang (partly in collaboration with the author and his family).

Young Amir and Hassan walk through Kabul-styled Kashgar

A street scene is filmed on location in Kashgar, chosen for its similarity to Kabul in the 1970s and 1990s

For most people, there is a clash between their image of Afghanistan and a rather monolithic image of China. Yet, even some of our Chinese crew (who had come from Beijing) were struck by how removed Central-Asian Kashgar was from the Chinese cities in which they had grown up.

I remember the children on our film who had become homesick in the short period we spent in Beijing before heading west. When they arrived in Kashgar, that homesickness suddenly disappeared: they were in Central Asia again. For me, as for them, various parts of the city bore an uncanny similarity to the Afghanistan we had just left – particularly the old city in which we shot many of our kite-flying scenes. Foodwise, though, they would complain that the kebabs in Kabul were much better, and I agreed.

In Kashgar, Khaled and his father came to visit the set. He was an immensely supportive presence throughout all stages of filmmaking, and he and David Benioff, the screenwriter, would exchange many late-night emails discussing the book and Afghan culture. Throughout, he was there for advice, if needed. And the two weeks spent with us on set were as special for him as they were for us. The world of his book, which until then had existed only his imagination, suddenly became real. With us, he walked into Baba's house, and he could see aspects of his book talking back to him. Time and again he would say how much our sets reminded him of his childhood.

The first time he watched me act, I was terrified that he would not feel I was up to scratch. That evening, he took me aside with some very kind words, and when he left Kashgar, he gave me a signed copy of *The Kite Runner* and wrote inside: 'You are Amir' – clearly, very dear words to me. Indeed, to all of us, Khaled said that whenever he looks back at the book and thinks of the characters, he only sees us.

For me, one of the greatest attractions of *The Kite Runner* as a project was the fact that it is a family story. I was very aware that this would be the first major Western studio film in which the primary point of contact with Afghanistan (and the Middle East) was a human story as opposed to one of political violence. When people think of Afghanistan, *burqas*, the

Taliban, terrorism and bombs come to mind. Rarely does anything positive resonate, and rarely is the emphasis on a shared humanity. The opportunity to work on something that would help reverse a long stream of stereotypes and simplifications made me very eager to be involved. Afghanistan once had the largest refugee population in the world, numbering six million. Therefore, the story of the Afghan refugee is the story of refugees the world over – one reason why, I think, *The Kite Runner* appeals to so many people.

I plan to return to Central Asia. I love the majesty of the landscape and the feeling of being at a crossroads of civilisations. Standing at the head of a valley or on the side of a mountain and allowing a Romantic sensibility to overtake me, I could imagine the armies of Alexander or the Mongol hordes passing through. It is a land that has been invaded by just about everyone, for better or worse, but the range of colours and the mix of races is something I adore. Yet so few people know anything about the region. Afghans living in the West say that before 2001, if asked about their origins, they had to explain where Afghanistan was. But while filming, we were among Afghans wherever we went. One of the most valuable experiences I took with me from working on this film was the opportunity to have travelled within a community that way. □

The Kite Runner was released on DVD in the US in March 2008. It will be released in the UK in June 2008.

Khalid Abdalla studied English Literature at Cambridge University and starred in the 2006 Academy Award-nominated film *United 93*. He is currently working on a film with director Paul Greengrass about the first two months of the invasion of Iraq in 2003.